A N
INVITATION TO

Social
Psychology

EXPRESSING AND CENSORING THE SELF

Dale T. Miller
Stanford University

THOMSON

™

WADSWORTH

Australia • Canada • Mexico • Singapore • Spain
United Kingdom • United States

Acquisitions Editor: *Michele Sordi*
Assistant Editor: *Dan Moneypenny*
Editorial Assistant: *Jessica Kim*
Technology Project Manager: *Erik Fortier*
Marketing Manager: *Chris Caldeira*
Marketing Assistant: *Nicole Morinon*
Marketing Communications Manager:
Tami Strang
Project Manager, Editorial Production:
Emily Smith

Art Director: *Vernon Boes*
Print Buyer: *Rebecca Cross*
Permissions Editor: *Joohee Lee*
Production Service: *Matrix Productions Inc.*
Text Designer: *Cheryl Carrington*
Copy Editor: *Victoria Nelson*
Compositor: *Integra*
Cover Designer: *Bill Stanton*
Text and Cover Printer: *Malloy Incorporated*

Printed in the United States of America
1 2 3 4 5 6 7 09 08 07 06 05

For more information about our products, contact us at:
Thomson Learning Academic Resource Center
1-800-423-0563

For permission to use material from this text or product, submit a request online at
http://www.thomsonrights.com.
Any additional questions about permissions can be submitted by email to
thomsonrights@thomson.com.

Thomson Higher Education
10 Davis Drive
Belmont, CA 94002-3098
USA

Asia (including India)
Thomson Learning
5 Shenton Way
#01-01 UIC Building
Singapore 068808

Australia/New Zealand
Thomson Learning Australia
102 Dodds Street
Southbank, Victoria 3006
Australia

Canada
Thomson Nelson
1120 Birchmount Road
Toronto, Ontario M1K 5G4
Canada

UK/Europe/Middle East/Africa
Thomson Learning
High Holborn House
50–51 Bedford Row
London WC1R 4LR
United Kingdom

Library of Congress Control Number:
2004118288

ISBN 0-534-59205-8

To my parents, Evangeline and William Miller

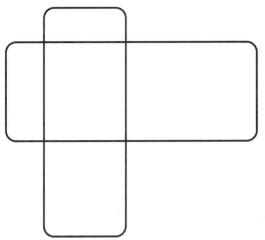

About the Author

Dale T. Miller is Professor of Psychology and Morgridge Professor of Organizational Behavior at Stanford University. Born in Canada, he received his B.A. from the University of Victoria and his Ph.D. from the University of Waterloo. Before joining the faculty at Stanford University in 2002, Miller held faculty positions at the University of Western Ontario, Simon Fraser University, University of British Columbia, and Princeton University. He has published articles in many different areas of social psychology, but his recent research has focused on the impact of social norms on social life. He is coeditor with Deborah Prentice of *Cultural Divides: The Social Psychology of Intergroup Contact* and with Michael Ross of *The Justice Motive in Everyday Life.* He has been a fellow at both the Center for Advanced Study in the Behavioral Sciences (Stanford) and the Institute for Advanced Study (Princeton). Miller has taught introductory social psychology for over thirty years.

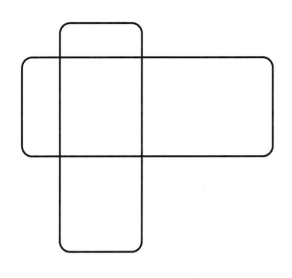

Contents

Chapter 3   Conformity   33

Chapter 4   Self-Censorship and the Collective   53

Chapter 5   Self-Censorship and the Individual   71

Chapter 6   Censoring and Expressing Prejudice   89

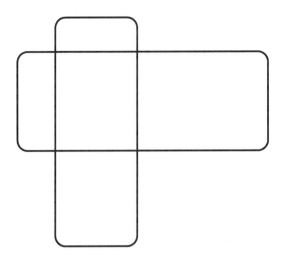

Preface

Can one learn a lot *about* social psychology without learning about a lot *of* social psychology? I believe one can, and this book is my attempt to prove it. Social psychology's mission is to illuminate social experience—from the everyday, who-would-have-noticed-that variety to the shocking, no-normal-person-would-do-that variety. That mundane and extreme forms of social behavior are more similar than dissimilar in their origins is a major theme of social psychology as well as this book.

In pursuing their mission, social psychologists employ a combination of traditional scientific tools (e.g., experimental manipulation and control groups) and more specialized tools of the social psychological trade (e.g., experimental cover stories and confederates). Conveying an appreciation of the craft of social psychology is one of my major goals for this book. For this reason, I have chosen to describe fewer studies but provide more details about them, especially those pertaining to their procedure and context, than is typical. There are reasons classic studies are classic, and I've tried to reveal those reasons in my description of them.

The material in this book is organized around the theme of self-censorship. I chose this theme because I believe that much of the most interesting research and theories in social psychology pertain in one way or another to the causes and consequences of people's acting or speaking in ways that contradict their private experience. Having written the book, I am even more convinced that this is true.

The theme of self-censorship provides the major storyline of the book, but I've also tried to let each of the studies described tell its own story. More generally, I have tried to write this book so that it would be interesting and accessible to those with little background in psychology as well as to more knowledgeable readers.

In Acknowledgment

Many people have contributed directly and indirectly to this book. I owe a great debt to my undergraduate teachers Ronald Hoppe and Alex Bavelas for piquing my interest in social psychology and for making me want to do it. I owe an even greater debt to my graduate mentors John Holmes, Mel Lerner, and Michael Ross for teaching me how to do it. Over the last 30 years my thinking about social psychology has benefited from innumerable colleagues and students, but it is Cathy McFarland and Debbie Prentice who have most deeply influenced my thinking about the ideas expressed in this book.

For graciously reading and providing a wealth of helpful comments on all or various portions of the book I am extremely grateful to Evan Morrison, Benôit Monin, Penny Visser, Rebecca Ratner, Maia Young, Nicole Shelton, Brian Lowery, Jacquie Vorauer, and Sarah Townsend. I also am appreciative to the following reviewers for their thoughtful feedback on earlier drafts of the book: T. William Altermatt of Hanover College; Melissa Atkins of Marshall University; Ozlem Ayduk of University of California, Berkeley; Mahzarin R. Banaji of Harvard University; Bruce Bartholow of University of Missouri, Columbia; Galen V. Bodenhausen of Northwestern University; Amy Buddie of Kennesaw State University; W. Keith Campbell of University of Georgia; Traci Craig of University of Idaho; Daniel DeNeui of Southern Oregon University; David Dunning of Cornell University; Sara Estow of Colby College; Adam Galinsky of Northwestern University; Anne Gordon of Bowling Green State University; Regan Gurung of University of Wisconsin, Green Bay; Robert Hessling of University of Wisconsin, Milwaukee; Sandra Hoyt of Ohio University; Alishia Huntoon of Washington State University; Jerald Jellison of University of Southern California; John Jost of New York University; Linda Kline of California State University, Chico; Benjamin Le of Haverford College; Deborah Prentice of Princeton University; Wayne Robinson of Monroe Community College; Gretchen Sechrist of University of Buffalo; Harold Takooshian of Fordham University; and Jacquie Vorauer of University of Manitoba.

Michele Sordi is owed special thanks for providing such wonderful editorial guidance throughout the project. Deep gratitude also goes to Kathy Oleson for the superb job she did with the end-of-chapter questions and research table appendix as well as with the instructor's manual that is available in electronic form from the publisher. The support offered by Princeton and Stanford Universities during the time I worked on this book was also a great boon, as was the luxury of a teaching-free year provided by the Institute for Advanced Study in Princeton.

My final and greatest debt is to Carol and Josh whose support and patience made the writing of the book, as so many other good things, possible.

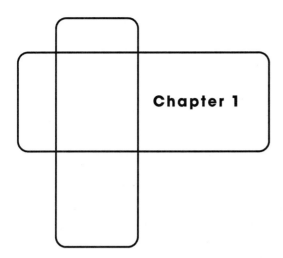

Chapter 1

Introduction

A sympathetic adult praises the drawing of an artistically untalented child

A terrified passenger allows her impaired roommate to drive her home

A bigoted employer hires a member of a minority group

A confused student pretends to understand a professor's lecture

A smitten young man conceals his feelings from the object of his affection

A stingy diner joins his more generous peers in leaving a large tip

A skeptical executive fails to voice her misgivings about her boss's decision

An offended coworker laughs off a peer's sexist comment

An alarmed pilot calmly informs passengers of an emergency landing

These behaviors, varied though they may be, all have one thing in common. They each involve individuals' taking public positions that diverge from their private experience. When people publicly conceal, disguise, or misrepresent their private feelings or beliefs, they are censoring themselves. Self-censorship, its causes, forms, and consequences, is the topic of this book.

As much as the book is about self-censorship, however, it is also about social psychology. As far as I know, no social psychologist has ever written a chapter, let alone a book, on the topic of self-censorship. Nevertheless, I contend that much social psychological research and theory focuses on self-censorship in one way or another. What follows is my attempt to make good on this claim. By organizing this book around the concept of self-censorship,

I hope to bring a fresh perspective to many of the most interesting topics—old and new—studied by social psychologists.

What is Self-Censorship?

We all know what censorship is. It involves one person's suppressing the words or actions of another. *Self-censorship* similarly involves the suppression of words or actions, but in this case the agent of suppression is the actor him- or herself. An employee whose superior suppresses her report of her company's illegal activity has been censored; an employee who decides to suppress her knowledge of her company's illegal activity for fear of peer disapproval has censored herself.

The value placed on freedom and individuality in our culture leads many to think that self-censorship is inherently undesirable—an act of weakness or cowardice that should be resisted. This assumption is unwarranted. Self-censorship is inherently neither good nor bad. Certainly, some acts of self-censorship reflect a failure of will, but others, as in the case of an alarmed pilot who conceals her fear from her passengers, reflect the presence of will power and bespeak courage rather than weakness. For people to successfully negotiate their social world, they must have the ability to suppress their private feelings and thoughts and, equally important, to disguise the fact that they are doing so. Recall the child-praising adult in the opening example. To achieve his goal of encouraging the child's artistic ambition, this individual must be capable of both withholding his true opinion from the child and concealing this deceit from her. Self-censorship is also essential to the smooth functioning of society. Civilized life would not be possible were people not both able and willing to censor their strongest antisocial feelings.

Social Psychology and Self-Censorship

The self-censorship process illustrates two of the most central themes in social psychology. The first of these is the claim that humans are norm followers; the second, that humans are meaning seekers.

Humans as Norm Followers

The regulation of social life requires that we be exquisitely sensitive to social cues and social norms. What we do and say in situations depends not simply on the feelings and thoughts that those situations arouse in us but on what we believe is appropriate. A common refrain among social psychologists is that situations (as opposed to stable internal aspects of people such as personality traits) are surprisingly powerful determinants of behavior. In fact, the phrase "the power of the situation" has attained the status of a mantra in the field (Ross & Nisbett, 1991).

In many cases, evidence that situational forces are powerful comes from the demonstrations of disconnects between people's public behavior and their private experience. That is, situations are often judged as powerful to the extent that they prevent people from acting upon their private feelings or beliefs. As we shall see in Chapter 3, for example, the most interesting cases of conformity usually involve circumstances in which people actually do not accept the behavior or attitudes of others but go along with them anyway. The power of peer pressure is never clearer than when the group induces its members to act differently without first getting them to think differently.

Humans as Meaning Seekers

Imbuing social experience with meaning is one of the principal tasks of the social actor. For it is the subjective meaning people attach to their circumstances, much more than the objective features of those circumstances, that guides people's actions. To claim that situations are powerful determinants of people's behavior is really to claim that people's interpretations or ways of construing situations are powerful determinants of their behavior.

Self-censorship provides a particularly revealing window into the process by which humans find meaning in their social life. First, the act of self-censorship is itself a response to the meaning that the person has imposed on a particular situation. A person's decision to censor him- or herself will only occur if that person has first attached a particular meaning to the situation. For example, unless people construe a situation as one in which the norm of fairness applies, they are unlikely to censor their more selfish impulses. Second, the act of self-censorship itself powerfully influences the meaning a situation has for the individuals. That a situation leads us to act in ways that diverge from our private experience will powerfully shape the meaning we attach to that situation. For example, seeing that we hesitate to speak our mind in a relationship conveys important information to us about that relationship. In sum, an act of self-censorship is both a response to a social situation and a component of that social situation.

Why Do We Censor Ourselves?

As the opening examples reveal, the motives behind self-censorship can vary widely. In extreme cases, self-preservation may be the motive. History and current events abound with examples of brutal regimes in which citizens' survival requires them to suppress their private beliefs. Saving one's life is rarely the motive behind self-censorship, however. Generally, self-censorship is prompted by social motives of one type or another, some of which are illustrated here.

To Preserve the Group and One's Standing in It

Two common motives for self-censorship are preserving the cohesiveness of one's group and preserving one's standing in it. Both of these motives can be seen at work in a recent study of eating practices on college campuses (Kitts, 2003). The focus of Kitts's study was student members of vegetarian houses. Not surprisingly, strong antimeat-eating norms existed in these houses, but members nevertheless varied considerably in how faithfully they practiced vegetarianism and the majority ate some type of meat (usually fish) on occasion. The students typically kept their meat eating private, however, and were careful not to let their housemates either see or hear about their meat eating. When asked why they concealed their carnivorous activities from their housemates, students cited concerns about both their own welfare ("I didn't want them to lecture me or make me feel guilty") and the welfare of their housemates ("I didn't want to gross them out").

To Enhance One's Attractiveness to Others

One reason that the vegetarian housemates in Kitts's study self-censored was to protect their social standing—they didn't want to fall out of favor with their peers. In other circumstances, people self-censor in order to promote, rather than merely maintain, their social standing, as a well-known study by Zanna and Pack (1975) illustrates. The participants in this study were undergraduate women who believed they were participating in an experiment to determine the accuracy with which people could judge another's personality from selected information about him or her. To this end, the participant and her fellow (temporarily absent) male participant were to exchange their answers to a series of personal questions from which they would form impressions of each other. Before the participant provided her answers, she received what were purported to be the answers of her partner. Included in this information was the fact that the partner's ideal woman either was home-oriented and deferential to her husband or was ambitious, strong, and independent. The information also signaled that the partner was either highly attractive or not.

As the experimenters predicted, the women described themselves differently depending on whom they thought they were going to meet. Women expecting to meet an attractive conservative male presented themselves as more traditionally feminine than women expecting to meet an attractive liberal male. This effect was less pronounced when the description of the man made him sound unattractive. Even more impressive, those women expecting to meet an attractive man with traditional views solved 18% fewer problems on an anagrams test than did those expecting to meet an attractive nonsexist man. They apparently did not want to scare the traditional male off by seeming too smart.

Of course, it is not only women who misrepresent themselves in order to impress attractive members of the opposite sex. Morier and Seroy (1994) replicated the Zanna-Pack experiment using male participants and found parallel results. Men are every bit as inclined as women to misrepresent the conservativeness of their sex-role attitudes in order to win the favor of an attractive member of the opposite sex.

To Avoid the Disapproval of Others

In addition to misrepresenting themselves in order to appear more attractive to others, people will also occasionally misrepresent the attraction they feel toward another, as a study by Bernstein et al. (1983) illustrates. This study recruited male college students for what was described as an investigation of people's reactions to classic silent films. The procedure supposedly required participants to watch a short clip from either a "sad clown" or "slapstick" silent film and provide reactions to it. The experimental room contained two desks with a television monitor situated on top of each. Two chairs, 3 inches apart, faced each monitor. A wooden partition separated the two desks and their accompanying chairs. When the participant arrived, he was told that the other participant, actually an assistant or "confederate" of the experimenter, was already set up. The confederate was an extremely attractive female. The experimenter told the participant that normally he would show different clips on each of the monitors but because one of the tapes was not working, in their session he was going to show the same clip on both monitors. The experimenter told the participant that he could sit wherever he liked—that is, either next to the female participant or in one of the chairs facing the other monitor.

One might expect that the men would choose to sit next to the attractive woman. In fact, only 33% of the men chose to sit with her, with 67% choosing to sit alone in the next cubicle. Does this mean that the men didn't want to sit with the attractive woman? To find out, consider the results from another condition in the experiment that paralleled the first in all respects except one: Here the movie clips shown on the two monitors were different rather than the same. When the males in this condition were given their choice of seats, they overwhelmingly (72% vs. 28%) chose the movie (which alternated across experimental sessions) that allowed them to sit next to the attractive woman. This result suggests that the men did want to sit next to the woman. So why did they not act on this desire in the one-movie condition? The likely reason they avoided sitting with the attractive female in that condition, despite wanting to do so, was their fear of how it would be interpreted by the experimenter and the woman ("Maybe she would think I was being too forward"). This concern and hence the motive to censor their true preference was not present in the two-movie condition (after all, who is to say that they didn't make their choice based on their attraction to the movie rather than their attraction to their cubicle mate?).

To Remain True to One's Self-Image

In the examples discussed thus far, the motivation for self-censorship has involved the reaction of others. In many cases, however, the relevant audience is the self. Consider the motivation to censor racist or sexist thoughts. As we will see in Chapter 6, people sometimes censor such thoughts because they fear that expressing them will provoke negative reactions from others, but they do so at other times because they wish to live up to their personal commitment to egalitarianism.

An interesting study by Daniel Batson and his colleagues (Batson et al., 1999) demonstrates how a personal commitment to fairness can lead people to censor impulses that are inconsistent with fairness. The experimental procedure was crafted so that participants were faced with the decision of how to allocate a valuable resource (who was assigned to which experimental task) between themselves and another participant. One of the tasks was designed to be much more desirable than the other—it was more interesting and it provided participants with the opportunity to win tickets for a $35 raffle. The experimenter led participants to believe that their partner would think that the task assignment was determined by chance.

Most participants (75%) responded to this opportunity in a self-interested manner and assigned themselves the desirable task. In another version of the experiment, participants faced a slightly more complicated situation. Here, before they were asked to assign the tasks, the experimenter said the following: "Most participants feel that giving both people an equal chance—by, for example, flipping a coin—is the fairest way to assign themselves and the other participants to the tasks." A coin was provided for participants to flip if they wished. Over half of the participants in this circumstance chose to flip the coin. It turned out, however, that deciding to do the "fair thing" and flip the coin did not mean that participants actually were fair, because approximately 85% of those who flipped the coin (in private) still assigned themselves to the positive condition. People wanted the desirable outcome for themselves, and when the fair procedure didn't yield it, they took it anyway.

The experimenters did find one way to induce participants to be fair, however: seat them in front of a mirror. This technique, strange as it may seem, is actually a common experimental means of inducing a state of self-reflection and inward focus in people. Looking into our own eyes apparently makes us reflect on who we are and what we stand for. Batson and his colleagues employed this technique to see if participants would be more likely to censor their selfish impulses and act in accordance with their personal commitment to fairness when they were made to focus inward. (The fact that most participants believed they should flip a coin suggests they believed in the principle of fairness.) The mirror did its job. Forcing participants to face, head on so to speak, the discrepancy between their avowed moral standard (be fair) and their standard-violating behavior (unfairly ignoring the result of the coin flip) was too much for them. Participants in this condition abided by the coin flip even when it dictated that they assign the favorable task to the other participant.

Does Self-Censorship Require Awareness?

Do people know when their public behavior gives false expression to their private psychological experience? Sometimes they do, but not always, as a study by Vorauer and Miller (1997) demonstrates. Undergraduate participants were recruited, two at a time, for an experiment purportedly concerned with determining the best research method for learning about students' college experiences. When the participants (who the researchers were careful to be sure did not know one another) arrived at the laboratory, they were told that they would be asked to answer a series of questions about their college experiences either on a highly structured questionnaire or in an unstructured verbal presentation. A coin toss determined which method they would use. At this point, the two participants were separated. During the 15 minutes when the first participant was completing his or her questionnaire, the second participant was told to collect his or her thoughts in anticipation of the presentation.

Just before the second participant was to begin describing his or her experiences in front of the first participant and a video camera, he or she was given a glimpse of the other's supposed questionnaire—actually one substituted by the experimenter. For half of the participants, this questionnaire provided a very positive depiction of the other student's experience; for the other half, a very negative description. Here's some of what they learned about the other participant in the negative condition.

"I guess I don't really feel like I have had very many positive academic experiences since I came here. . . . It's been much harder for me than high school was. . . . A couple of times when I've spoken up in class, I didn't think my ideas went over very well. . . . People usually seem to ignore or criticize what I say. . . . There is a lot of social pressure on campus. I actually think it is far worse than the academic pressure. . . . When I do go out, I tend to feel awkward, especially in groups."

Now imagine you were asked to describe your own experiences, both positive and negative, in front of the person you believed had written the description you just read. Do you think you would describe your experiences differently than you would have if you had just read a much rosier account of the other student's experiences? The behavior of the actual participants suggests you would. Despite being asked to spend an equal amount of time on their positive and negative experiences, participants spent significantly more time speaking about their negative experiences when they believed that the person they were speaking to had had a miserable college experience. What's more, they appeared unaware that they had matched the tone of the other's description. We can infer this because participants in the negative condition, like participants in the positive condition, actually reported that they had spent *more time* describing positive than negative experiences. They had censored their expressions of their experiences to be in sync with the other person but were unaware of doing so.

Consequences of Self-Censorship

Self-censorship generally facilitates the regulation of social life, but it occasionally yields costly by-products both for the individual and for the group. Social psychologists have a special interest in the unintended, collateral, "downstream" consequences of adaptive processes, so they have amply demonstrated the ways in which the self-censorship process can go awry.

Individual Consequences

Earlier we noted that under some circumstances self-censorship can save one's life; it can also cost one one's life and that of others, under some circumstances. Recall the opening example of the passenger who allows her impaired roommate to drive the two of them home. In Chapter 2 we will discuss the various reasons that people fail to be as assertive as they feel they should be in this circumstance, but for now let us simply observe the high risk people take when they do censor their cautionary impulses in this circumstance. True, the passenger may spare her roommate's feelings and avoid a scene, but the price for doing so can be extremely high for both. A missed opportunity for romance may be a less dire fate than perishing in a car accident, but the case of the young man who conceals his romantic feelings from the object of his affections provides another illustration of the unintended negative consequences that self-censorship can produce. Concealing his feelings may yield the short-term gain of sparing him the possibility of an embarrassing rejection, but, as in the previous example, it risks long-term pain.

Some of the most significant effects of self-censorship are the reactions people have to the experience of self-censorship itself. Having censored themselves, people may find themselves experiencing a wide range of emotions that are largely independent of the material consequences of their actions. For example, even if the impaired roommate safely negotiated the drive home, her compliant passenger may nevertheless experience painful self-recriminations for not having been more assertive. Conversely, the executive who overcomes her fear and expresses her misgivings to her boss may experience considerable pride even if her boss reacts negatively to her honesty.

The feelings that follow from the act of self-censorship are especially intense when others are present who act differently. Seeing others express their private thoughts and feelings when you censor yours will compound whatever good or bad feelings your actions aroused in you. Censoring the impulse to challenge another's sexist remarks may leave you feeling even worse if others spoke up; conversely, censoring the impulse to lash out at an error-prone new subordinate may leave you feeling even more virtuous if others prove unable to suppress theirs.

Collective Consequences

When all individuals in a social situation suppress their private feelings and beliefs, there can be additional consequences for the group as a whole. Recall the finding that most members of the vegetarian houses studied by Kitts concealed their meat eating from their housemates. The consequence of this widespread nondisclosure of private acts of norm violation was that all members of the houses, norm adherents and violators alike, underestimated the actual number of meat eaters in their midst by over 50%. This misperception no doubt had consequences for the individual house members—for example, norm violators may have suffered more guilt than they would have if they had known of the commonness of their "sin." But their nondisclosure likely also had consequences for the group as a whole. For one thing, the widespread underestimation of one another's comfort with meat eating may have produced stricter dietary policies than the majority of the house members wanted. Relaxing unpopular restrictions—against fish eating, for example—could never come to pass as long as the majority mistakenly assumed that others remained resolutely antimeat eating.

A tragic example of a collective consequence that followed from all members of a group censoring their feelings—in this case, of fear—occurred on September 11, 2001. Nearly half the deaths in the south tower of the World Trade Center on that day were at firms that had trading operations. One reason for the especially high fatality rate among these firms appears to be that the norms of trading units prevented the traders from either showing or acting upon their fears. "We were from a Wall Street mentality," said a vice president of a trading firm who was among the few who escaped from the 89th floor. "You're a trader. You're tough. You don't leave until the firemen order you to go. You don't leave the floor for anything, not even to go to the bathroom" (Moore & Cauchon, 2002, 11 September). Individual traders' suppression of any sign of fear or concern served to reinforce a collective aura of security and invulnerability. What kept the traders from leaving their offices, then, was not just their belief that they should appear fearless but their belief (based on the public nonchalance of their coworkers) that there was no cause for fear. We will examine more closely how situations like this arise in Chapters 4 and 5.

The Self in Self-Censorship

As a work about self-censorship, this book is ultimately about the self. The prominence of the self in self-censorship is obvious—it is both that which is being censored and that which is doing the censoring. But it is misleading to think of the "self" playing both the roles of the censor and the censored. More appropriate is to think of individuals as having multiple selves (Markus & Wurf, 1987) and of self-censorship as occurring when one of these selves dominates another.

Thinking of the self-censorship process as involving competition among multiple selves reveals an important truth: Self-censorship is not about people being inauthentic to some true self. Consider one of the examples with which we began the chapter. Is the self that believes that a young child's artwork is hideous any truer a self than the self that praises the work out of a wish to encourage the young child's artistic endeavors or the self that praises the work so as not to be seen as harsh by other adults? I think not. The self that is doing the censoring in the cases of self-censorship featured in this book is the *social* self–the self that strives to be accepted by and to coexist with others. This book does not show people being inauthentic, then; it shows them being social.

There certainly are times—for example, in about half of the situations described at the beginning of this chapter–when individuals and the groups to which they belong would be better off if they had censored the social self. Documenting, illustrating, and—most important–explaining these circumstances constitute one of social psychology's principle missions. Social psychology doesn't do these tasks to show the evils of the social self, however; it does them to show the existence of the social self. For never is it clearer that we are social animals than when we see—as we will throughout this book–the ease with which the social self dominates other selves.

Chapter Review

1. Describe at least one way in which self-censorship illustrates each of these ideas: (a) that people are norm followers, and (b) that people are meaning seekers.
2. Explain the following statement: Self-censorship is both a response to a social situation and a component of that situation.
3. Discuss four possible reasons that individuals might censor themselves. Under what conditions do you think each motive is most likely to come into play?
4. Provide an example of the consequences that self-censorship has for both individuals and social groups.

Going Beyond the Chapter

1. This chapter opens with nine examples of individuals' taking public positions that diverge from their private experience. Come up with a personal

experience that could be added as a tenth example. Using the framework set forth in the chapter, analyze this personal example.

a. Does your example suggest that you were a norm follower in this situation? A meaning seeker?

b. Why did you censor yourself? Do any of the four motives discussed explain your behavior?

c. What were the individual and collective consequences of your behavior?

2. The chapter suggests that individuals are sometimes unaware that they are censoring themselves. Do you think it is generally the case that people are unaware? Or do you think that individuals are aware that they are self-censoring yet are reluctant to admit it to themselves or to others? How could one distinguish actual lack of awareness from self-presenting that one lacks awareness?

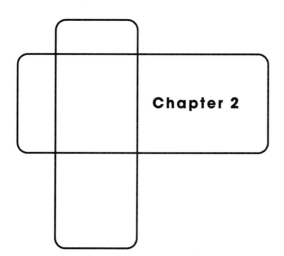

Chapter 2

Social Etiquette

Some years ago, Stanley Milgram and John Sabini (1978) conducted a study on the New York City subway. They wanted to see the reactions of passengers to someone who approached them and said, "Excuse me. May I have your seat?" This is a strange request (to say the least), because it violates a powerful social norm that Milgram and Sabini (1978) describe as follows:

> People get on the subway for a very clear and specific reason: To get from one place to another in a brief amount of time. The amount of interaction among the riders required for this purpose is minimal and the rules governing this interaction are widely adhered to. One rule of subway behavior is that seats are filled on a first-come, first-served basis. Another implicit rule is one that discourages passengers from talking to one another. Even though riders are often squeezed into very close proximity, they are rarely observed to converse. (pp. 32–33)

Because the request was so clearly illegitimate, you might predict that passengers would routinely rebuke the rule violator (actually undergraduate confederates of the researchers). Indeed, a group of people canvassed by the researchers predicted that less than 15% of the passengers approached would give up their seat. In fact, 56% of those approached gave up their seat, with another 12% sliding over to make room. In total, then, the confederates gained a seat almost 70% of the time they asked for one.

How can we explain the success of these rule-violating confederates? Why did passengers censor their undoubtedly strong impulse to deny the request made of them? It certainly cannot be attributed to the use of coercion. The confederates did not look menacing, and the researchers instructed them to avoid phrasing their requests as demands and to never question the passengers' rights to their seats. Why, then, was it so difficult for passengers to refuse this unreasonable request? The short answer is that passengers did not want to be impolite.

Implicit Social Etiquette: Respecting the Situational Definitions of Others

Although we normally think of rules of etiquette as applying to such things as utensil use, thank-you notes, and wedding protocols, such rules actually regulate behavior in all social situations. In the words of sociologist Erving Goffman (1959, 1971), rules of etiquette constitute the grammar or traffic rules of interaction.

One dictate of social etiquette is that we not challenge the claims people make about the situations they inhabit—their assumptions about what is and is not appropriate in that situation. Compliance with this injunction, which Goffman terms face saving, prohibits people from openly questioning another actor's understanding of a social situation as projected by his or her words and deeds. As Goffman (1959) states: "Under no circumstance is open conflict about the definition of the situation compatible with polite social exchange" (p. 150). Politeness requires that people avoid drawing attention to any actions of others that would embarrass them or question their adequacy as human beings, and this includes the definitional claims they make about the situations in which they find themselves (Emerson, 1970). In effect, challenging another's definition of the situation represents a moral reproach, something no properly socialized actor undertakes lightly (Sabini & Silver, 1982).

Let us return to the predicament of participants in Milgram and Sabini's study. By requesting the passenger's seat, the confederate communicated that he or she considered this action to be reasonable and appropriate. Thus, to deny the confederate's request for a seat would constitute a breach of social etiquette: It would directly challenge the confederate's apparent understanding that it was reasonable and legitimate for him or her to make this request. Even though the claim about the situation made by Milgram and Sabini's confederates no doubt struck most passengers as strange, they were inclined to give the confederate the benefit of the doubt—in effect, saying to themselves, "This cannot be as inappropriate as it seems."

Undoubtedly, an additional reason for the high compliance rate found by Milgram and Sabini was that passengers were caught off guard and probably found it difficult to produce a reason (at least a polite one) for saying no. Rather than risking impoliteness and a possible hassle by declining, passengers simply censored their desire to keep their seat. The results from another experimental condition reinforce this interpretation. In this condition the confederate's request was elaborated as follows: "Excuse me. May I have your seat? I can't read my book standing up." Only 42% of passengers complied with this request. By attaching a concrete reason (needing to sit down to read) to the request, confederates apparently resolved any ambiguity about the definition of the situation they were projecting, which allowed passengers to construe it as an illegitimate request. Confident of the illegitimacy of the request, passengers apparently concluded that it was no breach of etiquette to deny it. It was the person making the request who was violating etiquette, not them.

Compliance: When the Requestor's Definition Prevails

As ridiculous as the requests of Milgram and Sabini's confederates must have seemed to the subway passengers, the passengers were nonetheless fairly inclined to relinquish their seats. How general is this phenomenon, though? Do people usually comply with anything that anyone asks them to do? In fact, an entire field of study (see Cialdini, 2001) is devoted to identifying those variables that affect the likelihood that people will comply with requests—even unreasonable ones. These studies typically show that the likelihood of a request's leading to compliance depends upon many factors. Most interesting from the perspective of self-censorship, however, is the high rate of compliance these studies find in even their experimental conditions designed to elicit low compliance. Recall that in Milgram and Sabini's illegitimate request condition ("I can't read my book standing up") over 40% of the subway passengers gave up their seat. The frequency with which people comply with even unreasonable requests is truly astonishing.

Give Him a Nickel!

You are walking down the street and a person stops you, points to someone standing next to a parked car and an expired parking meter, and says to you, "This fellow is overparked at the meter and doesn't have any change. Give him a nickel!" How would you react? Brad Bushman (1988) conducted a study to find out. The setting was a street near a major shopping center in St. Louis, Missouri. The unwitting participants were 150 pedestrians who happened to walk along that street during the experiment. The experimenter positioned himself next to the parked car and proceeded to search his pockets for change. The confederate stood approximately 30 feet away from the car when he approached the chosen pedestrian.

This study had three experimental conditions defined by the clothing of the confederate. In the "no-authority" condition, the confederate was dressed as a panhandler in an old yellow T-shirt splattered with lavender paint, threadbare brown pants, and tattered tennis shoes. She was also carrying a plastic bag, suggesting that she might be collecting aluminum cans. In the "status-authority" condition, the confederate was dressed as a business executive in a formal dress suitable for professional wear, nylons, and dress shoes. In the "role-authority" condition, the confederate wore an ambiguous but highly distinctive uniform: dark blue pants and shirt.

Do you think the confederate's clothing would affect your reaction? The researchers assumed it would and predicted that someone who appeared to be in authority would be most successful in getting compliance. They were right: 72% of those approached by the confederate in a uniform gave a nickel, whereas only around 50% of the participants in the other two conditions complied. When they were asked by the experimenter why they came over and gave him a nickel, the vast majority of the compliant pedestrians indicated that they had accepted the confederate's definition of the situation—the most popular response being, "She told me to."

This is yet another situation in which someone does something that just isn't done. It may be legitimate to ask someone for a nickel, but it is not legitimate to *order* someone to give a nickel—at least not under most conditions. People who are confronted with this request probably will be confused and will search for a reason that a seemingly illegitimate request actually is not. Seeing the requestor's uniform will leave the pedestrian more comfortable on this score. We readily (if not happily) obey countless orders from ushers, policemen, and flight attendants that would provoke shock and consternation if they came from civilians.

It is interesting that the requestor's appearance affected compliance rates, but it is more interesting that the pedestrians so readily complied with the confederate's order (50% of the time) when she was dressed nondescriptly. Once again, people find it difficult to challenge someone else's definition of the situation—however bizarre that definition might seem.

The claim here is not that people always accept the social definitions of others—they do not. People often challenge the situational definitions of others and assert their own, but they do so with considerable reluctance. For example, consider how much easier it is to say to someone, "I'd prefer that you not smoke" when that person has first asked you, "Do you mind if I smoke?" than it is when he or she simply lights up. In some sense the distinction is puzzling, since one might be expected to sympathize more with someone who was polite and asked permission to smoke than with someone who disregarded others' preferences. Sympathy aside, however, it simply will be easier to voice one's preference to the former smoker than to the latter. By asking permission, the former is not only being polite but is also acknowledging the potential inappropriateness of smoking—thereby eliminating the bystander's worry that expressing her true preference would diminish or dishonor the smoker. On the other hand, the impolite smoker conveys a belief that her action is appropriate—and by challenging this definition, the bystander would risk insulting and demeaning her.

Salespersons regularly exploit the fact that people are reluctant to challenge another's definition of situations by using what are known as tag questions (Levine, 2003). A *tag question* is an assertion that ends with a request for confirmation from the listener. For example, the assertion might be, "This is a beautiful necklace," and the tag might be "... don't you think?" Think about it. How easy would you find it to respond to that sentence with something other than, "Yes it is," whatever you thought of the necklace? Not very, is it? The reason tag questions at the end of assertions of this type increase the likelihood that customers will verbally confirm the salesperson's claim (and therefore be more likely to buy the item) is that the act of denial comes with a deceptively high price—threatening the dignity or "face" of the salesperson.

Think how much easier it would be to disagree with the salesperson's assertion if he or she had said "I think this is a beautiful necklace. What do you think?" In this case, as in the earlier one, the salesperson has made the claim that the necklace is beautiful. The difference between the two statements is that in the first case the salesperson is communicating a much stronger presumption that his or her assessment is shared by the customer. As a consequence, any open disagreement with the salesperson's assertion would represent a much more serious challenge to him or her in the first case than the second. At least, this is what the salesperson is counting on.

Throwing a Frisbee in Grand Central

Darley and Latané (1970) conducted an intriguing field experiment that highlighted the power of social etiquette. They staged the experiment as follows: A female confederate sits on a bench in the waiting room at Grand Central Station in New York. Soon another female confederate sits down on a bench facing her; they pretend to recognize each other and begin a conversation. One has been shopping and announces that she has just bought a Frisbee. The other female asks to see it, and the first female throws it to her. They begin to toss the Frisbee back and forth. Apparently by accident, they throw it to a third person (also a confederate), and the reaction of this third person constitutes the experimental manipulation.

The study had three main conditions. In the control condition, the confederate did not join in the interaction but allowed the Frisbee to bounce off her accidentally and be retrieved by one of the two other females. The two females continued tossing the Frisbee back and forth and soon sent it to one of the 3–10 bystanders seated on the benches. They continued this until all the bystanders on the two facing benches had been probed. A bystander was counted as participating in the activity if he or she returned the Frisbee at least twice. By this criterion, 75% of the bystanders participated in the Frisbee tossing. This was approximately the same as the participation rate in a second condition (responsive-model condition) in which the confederate enthusiastically joined in. However, a very different participation rate occurred in a third condition (unresponsive model) where the confederate threw the Frisbee down, kicked it, and accused the two females of being childish. In this condition, none of the people subsequently thrown the Frisbee joined in. Instead, people sitting nearby would frequently move to other seats to avoid being thrown the Frisbee.

In each experimental condition, then, a different person defines the situation. In the control condition, the behavior of the first two females makes the claim that Frisbee tossing in Grand Central is perfectly reasonable. Thus it would be rude to discredit their definition and reject the Frisbee. In the responsive-model and unresponsive-model conditions, however, the action of the third female defines the situation. When she is responsive, she reinforces the confederates' definition that it is legitimate for bystanders to join them. When she is unresponsive, however, she projects the definition to both the two women and the other bystanders that participation is inappropriate. If the bystanders then joined in the game, they would discredit her definition and threaten her public image. An additional condition illustrates that the bystanders were indeed inhibited from acting on their desire to participate by the action of the third confederate. In this condition, the confederate was unresponsive but left the area once she had displayed her disgust for the idea of Frisbee tossing. The participation rate in this condition was almost as high (60%) as when the confederate had joined in. Clearly, the unresponsive confederate had not convinced the bystanders that it was inappropriate to participate—only that she thought it was inappropriate. Even if people privately enjoyed tossing the Frisbee, they were loath to challenge the confederate's situational definition in her presence.

The Used Water Bottle

The requests made in the foregoing studies may have been strange, but honoring them was not costly. Would people have been as willing to comply if the costs of doing so had been higher? In fact, people find it surprisingly difficult to discredit the situational projections of others—even when the failure to do so endangers them or others.

Martin and Leary (1999) provided an experimental demonstration of this fact. They sought to capture a situation in which one person offers to share a desired but possibly contaminated resource—in this case, a water container. Such an offer puts the thirsty person in a predicament. On one hand, this person wishes not only to quench his thirst, but also not to discredit the other's definition of the situation. On the other hand, this person likely wants to avoid drinking from a stranger's water bottle. After all, various infections and illnesses can be transmitted through sharing of beverage containers.

Martin and Leary's experiment was elaborate, but its bare bones were these: The experimenter told participants that she was investigating people's facial responses to bad tastes. The procedure required that one participant taste the liquids and the other (always the confederate) rate the taster's facial expressions. The experimenter gave the participant three small paper cups each containing 15 ml of liquid. The cups contained (a) a highly concentrated, unsweetened, peach-flavored soft drink; (b) a very salty mixture of soy sauce and table salt; and (c) a mixture of lemon juice and yellow mustard. Before the experiment was conducted, a panel of four tasters decided unanimously that the combined aftertaste of the three liquids was unpleasant but not so bad that participants had no choice but to accept the confederate's water.

After the participant had consumed the liquids, the experimenter said, "I'm supposed to have some bottled water for you to drink, but my assistant won't be here with it for another 15 minutes and for experimental reasons I can only give you bottled water. So I'm sorry, but I don't have a drink for you right now." As the experimenter turned her back on the participant and pretended to prepare questionnaires, the confederate reached into his backpack underneath the table and placed a 500 ml bottle of water in front of the participant. The clear plastic bottle contained 350 ml of water, making it look as if the confederate had already drunk from it. In reality, a clean bottle was used for each participant.

At this point, the confederate said one of two things. In one condition, he said, "That stuff must have tasted pretty nasty. Do you want a drink of my water?" In a second condition, he made the same statement but added: ". . . if you're not worried about drinking out of the same bottle as me." This latter wording was designed to increase the difficulty of rejecting the drink. Although there are fairly strong conventions against sharing food and food implements with a stranger (Rozin & Fallon, 1987), 35 of the 48 participants accepted the drink. Because of the generally high rate of acceptance, there was no difference across the conditions. However, there was a condition difference in the amount of water the participants drank. Participants consumed an average of 67 ml of water when the confederate raised the social costs of refusing but only 42 ml when he did not. It thus appears that the confederate shamed participants into drinking more than they wanted to by presenting the offer in such a way that to refuse would be rude.

Drinking and Driving

In real life, the risks people take to avoid challenging another's "face" are often much greater than we can capture in the laboratory. Imagine the following all-too-common situation. You have been at a social event, and when it is time to leave you realize that despite protestations to the contrary, the person who is supposed to take you home is too impaired to drive safely. We all know that the rational response in this situation is to try to discourage the person from driving and to find another means of getting home. This course of action, while rational, has a cost: It risks insulting the impaired driver by discrediting his or her definition of him- or herself as someone who is capable of driving. For this reason, people may seek to dissuade the would-be driver only gently and subtly, which may in turn embolden the driver to stick to his guns and insist that he is "perfectly capable" of driving. Although assurances of this type are not likely to allay your fears, they very well may make it more likely that you get in the car. The more assertively people defend their definition of the situation, the more impolite it is to discredit that definition. Be this as it may, any calculation that pits these two costs–potential loss of life and potential embarrassment–against one another would seem a "no-brainer." Surely people would not let their fear of offending someone put them in a life-threatening situation. Unfortunately, many of us have compromised our better judgment in such situations more than once.

To help better understand this analysis, consider the slogan "Friends don't let friends drive drunk." What is this message trying to accomplish? Is it trying to get people to stop others from drinking and driving by encouraging them to think of those at risk as friends? Possibly, but not likely. Rather, the point of the slogan seems to be redefining "real" friendship. Its message is that you are not being a friend by going along with your friend's projected frame that he or she is capable of driving. The slogan attempts to show that, in this context, true friendship is overcoming that reluctance to challenge friends' self-definitions. This campaign's very existence shows the difficulty of overcoming such reluctance.

It is certainly true that people can learn to challenge the self-definitions of others. Often people develop stock responses to situations involving inconsiderate smokers and overconfident impaired drivers that allow them to pursue the rational (if rude) course of action. Stock responses are especially likely to develop if people have confidence that another's situational definition (e.g., driving while impaired) is unreasonable and should not be honored. Thus, over time, we may learn how to summon up our courage and tell an impaired driver that we will not ride with her, just as we may learn over time to refuse second helpings of dessert. However, there will remain many novel situations in which people have not yet developed a practiced defense. In these situations, the fear of discrediting another's self-definition will retain a powerful and often destructive influence.

The Other Side of the Coin: The Pressure to Present Reasonable Definitions

The norm of respecting other people's situational definitions would not have such power were it not for a corresponding norm—that of presenting reasonable situational definitions oneself. Appropriately socialized actors do not make illegitimate claims about situations. People respect the projections of others because they assume that these projections are reasonable. In a sense, people abide by an implicit agreement both to respect one another's situational definitions and to present a situational definition worthy of respect.

The normative proscription against knowingly presenting an unreasonable definition of the situation explains why people don't routinely exploit others by asking for subway seats or anything else they want—most people find it difficult to intentionally make illegitimate requests. It may be quite easy to convince people that you are making a reasonable request (in your mind, at least), yet normative pressure prevents people from taking advantage of this fact. Indeed, it is often more difficult to make a norm-violating request than to refuse one.

This certainly seemed to be true of Milgram and Sabini's student confederates. According to Milgram and Sabini, the confederates reported "extreme difficulty" in carrying out the assignment. Students reported that while standing in front of a subject they felt anxious, tense, and embarrassed. Frequently they were unable to vocalize the request for a seat and had to withdraw. They sometimes feared that they were the center of attention in the car and were often unable to look directly at the subject. Once they made the request and received a seat, they sometimes felt a need to enact behavior that would make the request appear justified (e.g., mimicking illness, feeling faint). As a postscript, a journalist who interviewed Milgram and Sabini's confederates thirty years after the experiment found that they all still vividly recalled the discomfort their task produced in them (Luo, 2004, 14 September).

Projecting an inappropriate definition of their relationship to the passengers clearly left the student confederates very uncomfortable—and for good reason: They had breached social etiquette by doing something that an appropriately socialized person just does not do. This helps us understand why passengers on the subway found it so difficult to deny the confederate's request for their seat. They assumed that a normal person would not be psychologically capable of making this request of them without a good reason and thus they needed a good reason to say no. To state this more formally, *the likelihood of having a request complied with will be roughly proportional to the difficulty of making it.* As an example, to the extent that Milgram and Sabini's confederates would have found it easier to panhandle than to request a seat on the subway, those they panhandled should have found it correspondingly easier to say no.

Indeed, experience suggests that panhandlers are much less successful than were Milgram and Sabini's confederates—and people find it much easier to refuse panhandlers than they found it to refuse the confederates on the subway. Telemarketers are another segment of society whose requests are typically given less respect. Why do people consider it less rude to rebuff a panhandler? Why are telemarketers' requests considered less worthy of respect? Most likely, people do not see refusing such people as a challenge to the panhandlers' or telemarketers' definitions of the situation. Few people think that the requests from panhandlers and telemarketers reflect strong expectations of compliance. People do not assume that panhandlers and telemarketers have the right—or even that they themselves think they have the right–to expect that others will honor their request of money or time. Rejection may disappoint panhandlers and telemarketers, but it is not typically seen as degrading them.

Authority and Compliance:
The Milgram Experiment

The power of people's reluctance to challenge others' situational definitions assumed an ominous form in Stanley Milgram's (1974) seminal studies at Yale University in the early 1960s. Milgram advertised his studies as concerning the effects of punishment on learning. Three males participated in each session of the experiment: an experimenter, played by a 31-year-old high school teacher; a "learner" (victim) played by a 47-year-old accountant; and a "teacher," always destined by a fixed draw to be played by the real subject (a male ranging from 20 to 50 years of age). After an introduction and assignment of roles, the learner was placed in an electric chairlike apparatus and given an elaborate description of the nature of the task to be learned and the punishment delivery system.

The procedure was similar to many used in learning experiments at the time. The teacher was instructed to read a series of word pairs (e.g., *lion-tide*) to the learner and then after a specified interval to read the first word of each pair with four different second words (e.g., *lion: tide, time, team, test*). The learner was to indicate which of the four pairs had been previously presented. The learner was seated in the next room, and whenever he made an error (which occurred at predetermined intervals), the teacher (participant) had a panel with 30 levers, each of which corresponded to a designated voltage ranging from 15 to 450 volts. The teacher was required to increase the intensity of the shocks after each error. These various settings had verbal labels assigned to them: Slight Shock, Moderate Shock; Strong Shock; Very Strong Shock; Intense Shock; Extreme Intensity Shock; Danger: Severe Shock. The last two shock levers (435 volts and 450 volts) were marked XXX. To provide participants with an appreciation of the intensity of the punishment that could be administered, each teacher received a mild sample shock of 45 volts.

The learner, who of course did not really receive any shocks, activated a tape recorder that played a standardized sequence of screams and pleadings over an intercom. He pounded the wall and begged the teacher to stop, and eventually fell completely silent. If the teacher hesitated or questioned the procedure, the experimenter answered with one of four increasingly forceful prods:

Prod 1: Please continue, or Please go on.

Prod 2: The experiment requires that you continue.

Prod 3: It is absolutely essential that you continue.

Prod 4: You have no other choice; you must go on. (p. 374)

If the participant refused to continue after Prod 4, the experiment was terminated. No physical efforts were made to prevent participants from leaving if they got up or refused to push the shock buttons.

What did people do? Nine of the 40 participants stopped after hearing the pounding on the wall at 150 volts. But for most participants the experimenter's insistence overcame any misgivings they had about their own actions. Twenty-six of 40 participants (65%) continued until they had pressed the switch that administered the most intense shocks. They did this even though the experimenter had no special powers to enforce his commands, and even though their disobedience would not bring them any material loss or punishment.

If this finding shocks you, you are not alone. When Milgram (1974) asked people from all walks of life, including psychiatrists, how many people would obey the experimenter, they invariably predicted low obedience rates (with a maximal average shock of 130 volts).

Why Did People Shock?

To begin with, we can reject the hypothesis that Milgram's participants obeyed because they were mean or sadistic people. In a control condition in which participants were allowed to choose any shock levels they themselves considered appropriate, only two out of 40 people exceeded the 150-volt level and 28 never even went beyond 75 volts. Moreover, the obedient participants were clearly uneasy about the situation; profuse sweating, trembling, groaning, and nervous laughter were the norm. Many denounced the experiment as stupid and senseless and requested permission to stop.

Many factors likely contribute to the high level of obedience observed in Milgram's study. Milgram's (1974) own analysis placed great emphasis on the role of social etiquette. In his words,

> In order to break off the experiment the subject must breach the implicit set of understandings that are part of the social occasion. He made an initial promise to aid the experimenter, and now must renege on this commitment. Although to the outsider the act of refusing to shock stems from moral considerations, the action is experienced by the subject as renouncing an obligation to the experimenter, and such repudiation is not undertaken lightly. (pp. 149–150)

Milgram goes on to say:

> The experimental situation is so constructed that there is no way the subject can stop shocking the learner without violating the experimenter's self-definition. The teacher cannot break off and at the same time protect

the authority's definition of his own competence. Thus, the subject fears that if he breaks off, he will appear arrogant, untoward, and rude. Such emotions, although they appear small in scope alongside the violence being done to the learner, nevertheless help bind the subject into obedience. They suffuse the mind and feelings of the subject, who is miserable at the prospect of having to repudiate the authority to his face. The entire prospect of turning against the experimental authority, with its attendant disruption of a well-defined social situation is an embarrassment that many people are unable to face up to. In an effort to avoid this awkward event, many subjects find obedience a less painful alternative. . . . It is a curious thing that a measure of compassion on the part of the subject, an unwillingness to "hurt" the experimenter's feelings, is part of those binding forces inhibiting disobedience. The withdrawal of such deference may be as painful to the subject as to the authority he defies. (pp.150–151)

To the extent that fear of challenging the experimenter's projected image (face) is responsible for participants' willingness to obey him, we ought to find a substantial drop in obedience when the preconditions for the experience of these emotions are eliminated. This is precisely what occurred. In one of Milgram's experimental conditions the experimenter departed from the laboratory and gave his orders by telephone. When the participants did not have to challenge the experimenter's self-definition to his face, maximal obedience dropped to 21% (a number of participants said over the phone that they were giving higher shocks than they in fact did!). Thus much of the obedience shown by Milgram's participants was rooted in the face-to-face nature of the social occasion. As Milgram notes, participants acted as though there was some element of bad form in objecting to the destructive course of events or, indeed, in even making it a topic of conversation. Participants in the experiment most frequently experienced their objections as embarrassing. Even those who did refuse to continue felt embarrassed by it, saying such things as, "I don't mean to be rude, but I don't think I can continue."

Confronting Others in Their Own Space

People are more hesitant to challenge another's self-definition in some situations than in others. People are especially hesitant to challenge others in the others' own space. For example, in Milgram's study the experimenter "owned" the space and retained the right to define what was and was not unusual in that space. Similar examples include spaces such as airplane cockpits and hospital operating rooms. In these spaces it is the captain and the surgeon, respectively, who define what is normal, and it is especially difficult to challenge their definitions. This is the case even for those people whose job description compels them to do just that. Copilots, for example, have been shown to have a very difficult time questioning the captain's actions even when they feel that those actions are endangering the safety of the plane (Linde, 1988). They find it especially difficult to insist that the captain is in error if he or she resists when the problem is first brought to his or her attention. In one relevant study, Harper, Kidera, and Cullen (1971) found that over 25% of copilots in a simulation did not take control when the captain feigned incapacitation.

Similar problems can arise in operating rooms when a medical staff member notices problems of which the surgeon seems unaware—for example, that she is operating on the wrong side of the patient's brain. The detection of such errors is one of the reasons that so many staff are in attendance during surgery. But it is not always easy to challenge the surgeon's definition of the situation—and not just because people fear the consequences of doing so (Helmreich, 1997). One might not think that innocuous dinner-table errors such as having food on one's face have much in common with cockpit errors or operating room errors, but they do—in both cases people are reluctant to jeopardize the public image of others.

We all know that it is sometimes necessary to threaten the face or public image of someone who purports to be the authorized expert in a situation. The difficulty lies in knowing whether the situation in which you find yourself warrants it, especially in the heat of the moment. Those in cockpits and operating rooms who see things go wrong do not typically make a conscious decision to suppress their concerns. They usually will try to point the error out, though in doing so they will strive to minimize loss of face for the surgeon, captain, or authority. In some cases, they may simply expect and hope that the person will recognize the problem without intervention, just as people expect and hope that another will become aware of the tomato sauce on his chin.

The Etiquette of Prejudice and Discrimination

Most of the situations described thus far involve unusual circumstances. People do not demand that strangers give other people nickels, or relinquish their subway seats, or find themselves in psychology experiments delivering electric shocks to someone—at least not very often. Social etiquette also plays an important role in the nonnovel situations of everyday life. As an example, consider people's reactions to everyday instances of racism or sexism.

Prejudice Succumbs to Etiquette

A famous study conducted 70 years ago by the sociologist Richard LaPiere (1934) provides another example of people's compromising their convictions (in this case prejudiced convictions) in order not to violate social etiquette. LaPiere was interested in prejudice toward Asians, which was considerable in California at the time he conducted his study. Over a two-year period, LaPiere and a young married Chinese couple visited 184 restaurants and 67 hotels, auto camps, and tourist camps. Sometimes all three of them went into the establishment, sometimes the Chinese couple went in first. The couple was refused service only once, at an auto camp. Clearly, these businesses' actual practices showed no evidence of anti-Chinese prejudice. Neither did the interpersonal treatment the couple received. LaPiere coded the reception accorded the couple as hesitant, normal, or better than normal and he found that the couple received normal or better than normal treatment 90% of the time.

LaPiere discovered a very different picture when he sent a questionnaire to these and other establishments, asking (among other questions), "Will you accept members of the Chinese race as guests in your establishment?" Of the 256 establishments that returned the questionnaire (128 of which he and the couple visited previously), only two declared that they would accept Chinese guests unconditionally, and 18 said that they might depending on the circumstances. Thus, whereas more than 99% of the first sample accepted Chinese guests, more than 93% of the second sample (which included members of the first sample as well as new individuals) declared in writing that they would not do so.

Why did the desk clerks observed by LaPiere admit a Chinese couple to their establishments when they said they would not? According to LaPiere's analysis, this is another example of the power of social etiquette. LaPiere pointed to the important role played by the "air of self-confidence" that the couple exuded as they made their request. This projected self-image and the normative obligation it incurred proved much more powerful than the desk clerks' attitudes. In LaPiere's (1934) words, "A supercilious desk clerk could not refuse his master's hospitality to people who appeared to take their request as a perfectly normal and conventional thing" (p. 235). In effect, although refusing accommodation to a Chinese couple might or might not have constituted a social impropriety, refusing accommodation to a couple (Chinese or otherwise) who clearly defined themselves as deserving of it certainly did—it would have violated their self-definition.

Etiquette Succumbs to Prejudice

All of us have witnessed remarks that we feel are undeniably racist or sexist. The question we face in such situations is the following: Do we confront the speaker and point out the offensiveness of the remark, or do we let it pass? Janet Swim and Lauri Hyers (1999) created an experimental context in which female college students faced just this dilemma. Participants were recruited to participate in a group decision-making task. The experimenter escorted one participant and three confederates to a group discussion room where they were asked to sit in preassigned seats.

The participants' task was to select 12 individuals from a list of 15 women and 15 men with different occupational titles who would be best suited to survive on a desert island. The experimenter asked group members to take turns in a clockwise order, indicating their suggestion and a reason for their suggestion. She asked one of the confederates to record the group's selections. Thus, participants took part in the group discussion while the confederates made scripted comments. The male confederate sitting to the participant's right made either three sexist or parallel nonsexist statements during the group discussion. For example, during his final turn the confederate selected a female musician and in the sexist condition said, "I think we need more women on the island to keep the men satisfied," whereas in the nonsexist condition he said, "I think we need more musicians on the island to keep everyone happy." The confederate made these comments to the group as a whole and did not look at the participant when he made them. The other two confederates were instructed not to respond to the sexist remarks or to any other comments the participant might make about the remarks. After the 12 individuals were selected, one of the confederates informed the experimenter that the group had finished the task. The experimenter then led the participant and the confederates to private rooms to complete a questionnaire.

To assess the participants' reactions to the confederate's sexist comments, the researchers videotaped the interaction, and trained raters listed all the participants' verbal responses to the sexist comments. They also showed the videotapes to the participants, allegedly to help them recall their thoughts and feelings during the session. The experimenter instructed participants to stop the tape whenever they remembered having a thought or feeling during the session and to write it down. After participants finished viewing the tape, they were instructed to rate their thoughts and feelings on several dimensions.

The researchers were successful in creating a situation that women considered offensive. When the researchers described the experiment to a group of women, most of them said they would find the comments highly offensive. Indeed, 81% indicated that they would confront the target over at least one of his remarks. But what did the actual participants do? First, only 11% of the women confronted all of the sexist comments. In fact, only 45% confronted even one of the remarks. The majority offered no comment at all. When the women did confront the confederate, only 16% did so with direct verbal comments, such as indicating that the remarks were inappropriate or that the confederate should retract them. The most frequent style of confrontation was indirect, such as asking the confederate to repeat himself, asking rhetorical questions (e.g., "What did you say?") and registering surprise (e.g., "Oh my God, I can't believe you said that!").

Why didn't more women confront the sexist confederate—even indirectly? The women certainly considered the confederate sexist: In the postsession questionnaire, 75% described the confederate as prejudiced and 91% reported having negative thoughts and feelings about him. Many even readily admitted that they thought about confronting him: While viewing the videotape, most women privately mentioned having thoughts of confronting the confederate; moreover, in most cases these thoughts involved direct action such as arguing, name calling, scolding, leaving, and even hitting the confederate. Thus, most women experienced strong emotional reactions to the sexist comments but tended to censor them.

So why did roughly three times as many women indicate that they would comment on the inappropriateness of the remark than actually did? And why did a full 55% ignore the comments when none of the women predicted that they would? Ratings of the different response options by a separate group of women provide some insight. These participants were asked to rate various aspects of the different response options, including the extent to which it represented a risky response in terms of how the sexist person or others would react, and how polite or socially acceptable the response was. Obviously, one reason not to confront someone is concern about how the other might react. Interestingly, however, observer women's ratings of the riskiness of a particular response did not predict participant women's likelihood of actually engaging in a particular action—indicating that a woman's likelihood of taking action did not depend on her fear of the other participant.

Women's likelihood of choosing a particular response *was* predicted by their perceived politeness of the response: If women saw the response as impolite, they were less likely to choose it. Thus it appears that observer women underestimated the constraining power of the fear of impoliteness. It is surprising that women could even differentiate the range of responses in terms of politeness, given the nature of the offense. Because people evaluate response options in social situations (including even the Milgram situation) in terms of politeness, they are extremely reluctant to engage in an impolite action, no matter how justified they think that action might be.

Summing Up

One of the most important rules of social interaction—the violation of which is invariably disruptive—dictates that social actors avoid challenging the public "face" of others. Compliance with this injunction prevents people from openly questioning another actor's definition of a social situation as projected by his or her words and deeds. People's hesitancy to morally reproach another for his or her definition of the situation produces self-censorship of various forms. For one thing, it often leads people to comply with requests that they think are unreasonable, as occurred in Milgram's research. For another, it often leads people to stand silent when they witness someone else acting in a way they think is inappropriate or even dangerous.

These and other instances of self-censorship borne of etiquette concerns are especially likely to occur in unfamiliar and ambiguous situations. The more confident people are that the situational definition projected by another is unreasonable, the less likely they are to honor it. However, deciding that another's definition is unreasonable, or at least so unreasonable that it warrants challenge, is not always easy. People often find themselves in ambiguous and uncomfortable situations where the only thing they know for sure is that by speaking their mind they will violate social etiquette—and so they don't. Even having confidence that another's definition of the situation is inappropriate will not always embolden people to mount the necessary challenge, because doing so would still constitute a moral reproach. As when confronted with a person whose fly is unzipped or whose chin is besmeared, people often hold their tongue and hope that the situation will be righted without their having to do anything that would lead the other to lose face.

Chapter Review

1. Define Goffman's notion that individuals want to respect or at least not to challenge another's definition of the situation.
    a. Use both Milgram and Sabini's study and the idea of "tag questions" as examples of Goffman's idea.
    b. Consider how the idea that people have an implicit agreement to present reasonable definitions of the situation fits into this definition, again using Milgram and Sabini's work and the case of tag questions as examples. Do we expect salespersons, strangers, and friends to make this implicit agreement?
2. Use Darley and Latané's Frisbee study to illustrate the power of social etiquette. What are the definitions of the situation in each of the four conditions? How do participants' responses in each condition reflect the influence of social etiquette? Compare participants' responses across the conditions to build your argument.
3. Drawing on Martin and Leary's study and on the example of a drunk friend offering a ride, describe how respecting others' definitions of situations may prove to be personally costly.
4. Describe the key findings in Milgram's shock experiment. Why did participants respond as they did? How do we know that the participants were not evil individuals who responded in ways that others (like ourselves) would not have responded?
5. Compare the responses of LaPiere's participants when confronted with a Chinese couple asking for service and when asked by letter if they would serve Chinese individuals. What explains the diverging reactions?
6. Describe women's public behavior in Swim and Hyer's study when a male participant made sexist comments. Contrast this response with their private behavior when watching a videotape of their earlier interaction. Explain the differences in their behavior, drawing on the observations of other women who saw the videotape.

Going Beyond the Chapter

1. Brad Bushman finds that individuals are more apt to give a nickel when asked by a woman in an uniform ("role authority") as opposed to a woman dressed as a panhandler ("no authority") or as a business executive ("status authority"). While reading about this study, you may have been surprised that participants were not more likely to help when confronted with the business executive than with the panhandler. Why do

you think that there were no differences between these conditions? Why does the style of dress in the three conditions lead to different reactions? Do you think that there are additional factors (other than social etiquette) leading to the varying reactions?

2. This chapter asserts that "the likelihood of having a request complied with will be in direct proportion to the difficulty of making it." Test this contention with personal examples: Come up with a list of at least five possible requests. Then ask a friend to rank these requests in terms of the likelihood that someone will comply with them. Compare this ranking to your own ranking of the difficulty of making the requests. Do the rankings line up as the chapter would predict, with the most difficult-to-make requests leading to the highest likelihood of success? If not, are there other factors that seem to predict the likelihood that the requests will be successful?

3. Milgram suggested that social etiquette was a key factor influencing his participants' shocking (literally) behavior. However, as noted in the chapter, many factors were probably at work on their behavior. Examine the specific features present in Milgram's study and then predict whether varying the features would affect the level of obedience. For instance, imagine that participants were asked from the beginning to deliver a 450-watt shock. Do you think that they would have? Does it seem likely that the gradual nature of the increase in shocks contributed to participants' obeying the experimenter? What level of shocking would you predict if, instead of one experimenter, there were two who disagreed about what the participant should do? What if participants were in the same room with the victim of the shock and had to press the victim's hand on the shockplate rather than being in a separate room where they could not see the learner? Consider how features of the situation contributed to the obedience and in what ways the social etiquette account explains (or does not explain) the impact of these features.

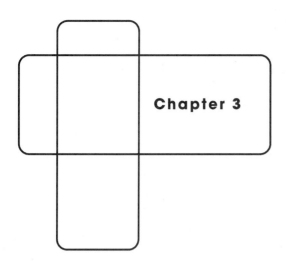

Chapter 3

Conformity

Americans had to watch their words in the immediate aftermath of the attacks on the World Trade Center in New York City and the Pentagon in Washington, D.C. on September 11, 2001. Those politicians who did speak out against the Bush administration's handling of the war or its legislative agenda were subject to intense hostility, including death threats. Dissent in the media was also subject to intense opposition. Two newspaper columnists in Oregon and Texas were fired for writing columns in which they asserted that President Bush's failure to return to Washington immediately after the bombing was cowardly. Advertisers pulled their ads from the TV show *Politically Incorrect* when its host challenged the president's characterization of the terrorists as "cowards"—the network then required the host to apologize. Even the college campus–that bastion of free speech—was not safe for politically incorrect speech. One academic of the Vietnam War generation was sanctioned by his university's administrators for reportedly saying, upon hearing of the attacks, "Anybody who can bomb the Pentagon gets my vote." Finally, even talk show hosts refrained from making jokes about the president for some time after the attack—a concession of no small consequence given the degree to which such shows depend on political irreverence.

Because speaking one's mind can be perilous when one's beliefs clash with those of others, people often censor deviant beliefs, either by holding their tongues or by misrepresenting their true beliefs. Consider the plight of those who hold religious beliefs that clash with majority views. One of the most notorious instances of religious persecution occurred in seventeenth-century Spain during what has come to be known as the Spanish Inquisition. Specifically, Muslims and Jews were threatened with death if they did not convert to Catholicism. At the same time that non-Catholics were forced to conceal their religious convictions in Spain, Catholics were concealing their faith from authorities in England, under whose laws Protestantism was the sole legitimate religion. Colonial America saw its own share of religious intolerance and persecution of dissent. Here is how one historian described the fate of the religious deviant in New England (cited in Kuran, 1995):

> Those who did not hold with the ideals entertained by the righteous. . . . had every liberty . . . to stay away from New England. If they did come, they were expected to keep their opinions to themselves; if they discussed them in public or attempted to act upon them they were exiled; if they came back, they were cast out again; if they still came back, as did four Quakers, they were hanged on Boston Common. And from a Puritan point of view, it was good riddance. (p. 99)

Those with deviant political opinions have met similar danger. The history of those who have been jailed, tortured, banished, and killed for speaking their political minds is too familiar to require retelling. Stifling political dissent is most common and most brutal in authoritarian or totalitarian regimes, but as the opening example illustrates, it even occurs, at least in periods of threat, in countries with strong traditions of free-speech protection like the United States.

Punishing Opinion Deviants

Investigations of psychological reactions to deviance suggest that there are frequently two stages in the majority's response to those who express deviant positions. First, majority members attempt to persuade deviants to change their ways or beliefs. If this attempt fails, the majority then excludes or punishes the deviant. Stanley Schachter (1951) conducted the most famous experimental demonstration of this phenomenon.

Conformity Pressure in the Laboratory

Schachter's participants were college students who had expressed interest in joining a "club" to advise on the treatment and disposition of delinquents, sex offenders, and the like. The club "meeting" consisted of five to seven male students, a leader (the experimenter), and three confederates. Following preliminary introductions, each member read a brief life history of a juvenile delinquent, Johnny Rocco. The case, which was presented as that of a real person, ended as Johnny awaited sentence for a minor crime. When the members had read the case, the leader asked them to discuss and decide the answer to the question: "What should be done with this kid?" Participants indicated their recommendations on a seven-point scale ranging from (1) lenient treatment, emphasizing love and affection, to (7) very severe treatment, including incarceration. Once the participants and then the confederates had announced their recommendations, the group engaged in a 45-minute discussion.

The participants generally took a middle position on the scale, advocating some mixture of love and punishment. The three confederates each played a unique role in the discussion: The *deviate* advocated extreme punishment and maintained his position throughout the discussion. The *slider* also advocated extreme punishment at the beginning of the discussion, but shifted and adopted the prevailing moderate view midway through the discussion. The *conformist* adopted the moderate opinion from the very beginning and maintained it throughout the discussion.

Schachter was especially interested in the communication patterns within the group—who communicated with whom. To gain insight into these patterns, he had an assistant take notes during the discussion. The results were surprisingly clear: There was a rather uniform level of communication directed toward the conformist throughout the discussion, a tendency to reduce communications to the slider as he fell in line, and a tendency to direct frequent communications toward the deviate, at least until near the end of the discussion. Most group members eventually gave up on the deviate but not before trying very hard to bring him into line.

From members' postdiscussion opinions of one another, it appears that the cessation of communication with the deviate reflected rejection rather than admiration or indifference. The collection of the postdiscussion measures was justified to participants by telling them that it might be necessary to reduce the number of club members or to break up the group, and thus it would be helpful to know which people would like to remain together. Participants were asked to rank the other group members in order of preference. Not surprisingly, the conformist, who tried to act like the average group member, received ratings similar to those received by the average group member. More interestingly, the slider also received average ratings—suggesting that the group members did not hold his initial disagreement against him. As long as one can be made to see the error of one's ways, all appears to be forgiven. No such charity was extended to the deviate—he consistently received the lowest ratings.

Other research also shows that group members reject those who adopt deviant positions within the group (Levine, 1989). Jonathon Freedman and Anthony Doob (1968) provided one such demonstration. They convinced a group that one of its members had consistently conformed to, and another had consistently deviated from, its norms. The group was then asked to pick two of its members to take part in additional experiments. In one, the partici-pants would receive money; in another, the participants would receive electric shock. Guess who got picked for which experiment? You got it! The group chose the conformer for the money experiment and the deviant for the shock experiment. Failing to go along can be costly.

Conformity Pressure in the Courtroom

The situation facing participants in Schachter's experiment paralleled that fac-ing jurors in many respects; thus, it should not be surprising that there have been many documented cases where "hold-out" jurors have been bullied and ridiculed for their dissenting positions. One example of such pressure comes from an in-depth analysis of a real-life jury conducted by Victor Villasenor (1977). The trial of Juan Corona, who was accused of serial murder, was long and involved a great deal of information and conflicting testimony. Villasenor attempted to reconstruct the eight days of deliberations from an extensive set of interviews he conducted with the jurors.

The vote taken on the first day revealed five jurors favoring a guilty verdict and seven an innocent verdict. Over time, the number of jurors favoring a guilty verdict steadily increased. The deliberations became intense on day 6, at which time the vote was 9–3 favoring a guilty verdict. Strong pressuring of the three-person minority by the nine-person majority ensued, and a vote taken at the end of the day was 11–1. At this point, the pressure put on the lone holdout was intense. Much of the pressure on her focused on the merits of the case, but much did not. This is clear from the comment she made when she finally succumbed to the pressure and changed her vote to guilty: "Please, I'll change my vote. Just don't hate me." Many other examples exist of jurors who have admitted capitulating under group pressure (see Smith & Mackie, 2000).

Conformity in the courtroom is not confined to the jury box. Evidence suggests that it may actually extend to the judge's chambers (Sunstein, 2003). Judges are meant to apply the law objectively, but it is commonly recognized that judges' ideologies influence their decisions. In ideologically contested cases (e.g., those pertaining to environmental regulation, affirmative action, or gender discrimination), a good predictor of a federal judge's vote is often the political party of the U.S. president who appointed him or her (Cross & Tiller, 1998). In the case of the three judge panels, however, an even better predictor of a judge's vote is often the political party of the U.S. president who appointed the other judges. This means that a Republican appointee on a panel with two Democratic appointees tends to vote in less stereotypical Republican manner than one on a panel with two other Republican appointees. Democratic appointees are similarly affected by the ideology of their fellow panel members. In fact, a Republican appointee sitting with two Democratic appointees tends to vote more liberally than a Democratic appointee sitting with two Republican appointees. No evidence at this point sheds light on how conformity pressures are exerted in the judge's chambers, but the data on vote convergence leave little doubt it occurs.

Conformity Pressure in the Cabinet Room

Even high-ranking government officials are subject to punishing social pressure techniques when they express opinions with which their colleagues disagree. Irving Janis (1982) provides many such examples in his analysis of foreign policy decisions and fiascoes. Consider one case, described by Thomson (1968) (cited in Janis, 1982) that occurred in the Johnson administration during the Vietnam War. According to Thomson, every senior official in the hierarchy was subjected to conformity pressures. Specifically, those who openly questioned the escalation policy were made the butt of an ominous epithet: "I am afraid he's losing his effectiveness." Dissenters often then suppressed or toned down their criticisms out of fear of being branded a has-been and losing access to the seats of power. The social pressures by which dissenters were neutralized—or "domesticated," in the language of the Johnson White House—could be quite subtle, as one "domesticated dissenter" and close adviser of President Johnson, Bill Moyers, discovered. When Moyers arrived at a meeting, Thomson tells us, the president greeted him with "Well, here comes Mr. Stop-the-bombing." At other times Johnson referred to him as "our favorite dove."

Punishing Behavioral Deviants

Behavior that violates the law is subject to formal punishment. Behavior that is legal but nevertheless violates group norms is subject to informal punishment.

Conformity Pressure in the Classroom

Every student is familiar with norms pertaining to the appropriate level of academic achievement or effort. Before Ivy League campuses went coeducational, the prescribed level of academic achievement was captured by the phrase "gentleman's C." This phrase reflected an important campus norm: It was ungentlemanly to receive grades either higher or lower than Cs. Norms have changed since the days of the gentleman's C; for one thing, professional and graduate schools now require more than a C average; for another, grade inflation has occurred. Though the concept of the gentleman's C may be outmoded, the idea that working too hard renders a student uncool still exists.

One extremely effective way of bringing overachieving students (or deviants of any other sort) into line is to taunt them with epithets. Names categorize and exclude those to whom they are applied and so are powerful deterrents to norm-violating behavior. The term *brown noser* is one time-honored epithet that generations of students have used to keep overly ambitious peers in line.

Guinier, Fine, and Balin (1997) found that one way that male (and some female) law students discouraged female students from speaking up in class was through "lesbian-bating"; that is, women who spoke more in class than was considered appropriate for their gender (members of which, it appears, are meant to be seen but not heard) were labeled "man-hating lesbians." Sadly, this informal punishment strategy was effective. As one female student at the University of Pennsylvania Law School told the investigators: "After I discovered I was being called a feminazi dyke, I never spoke in class again" (p. 54).

What is interesting about the last example is that students are not punishing peers for being homosexual—though gays and lesbians obviously have been and still are punished for their sexual orientation. Instead, students are punishing peers by *calling* them homosexual. Of course, it is not just in the academic realm that epithets regulate behavior. Youths are goaded into many actions by their fear of being labeled squares, dweebs, scrubs, and so on.

Conformity Pressure in the Workplace

The manufacturing boom that occurred after World War II produced great interest among social psychologists in the determinants of worker productivity. One factor that these investigators repeatedly found to be important was worker enforcement of social norms pertaining to their productivity. The level of productivity in a work group depended less on what was humanly possible than on what the group considered socially acceptable. Coch and

French (1948) conducted one of the best-known studies in this tradition at the Harwood Manufacturing Company. Their investigation soon uncovered a norm that prescribed how many units a worker was expected to produce per hour. A worker who failed to meet or exceeded this quota got in trouble. Those who worked below the norm were pressured to increase their productivity; those who worked above it were pressured to reduce it. Specifically, deviants were given the silent treatment or taunted with epithets such as "rate buster" and worse.

Conformity Pressure on the Street Corner

Overperformance is subject to peer pressure even when the activity in question is not central to the objectives of the group. William Foote Whyte (1943) provides a classic example of this phenomenon with his study of youth gangs in an Italian section of Boston during the 1940s. His analysis of what he termed "street corner society" (groups of mostly unemployed men in their twenties) devoted considerable attention to the interpersonal relations within the groups.

Perhaps the most vivid case of social influence in Whyte's study concerned the influence that group members exerted in one of the group's favorite activities—bowling. Group members varied in their status within the group, and their bowling scores tended to match their level within the status hierarchy. The highest-status members in the group also tended to be the group's best bowlers. It was not clear how this relationship emerged, but it was clearly reinforced through social pressure. If one of the lower-status members began bowling well, he was razzed and harassed until his score fell. "Doc," the highest-status member of the group, vividly describes (Whyte, 1943) what would happen if a low-ranking player bowled well: The lowerranking bowlers "wouldn't have known how to take it. . . . If they had won, there would have been a lot of noise. Plenty of arguments. We would have called it lucky—things like that. We would have tried to get them in another match and to ruin them. We would have put them in their places" (p. 61).

The (Un)Popularity of Deviants

People who express deviant opinions or violate social norms are not always punished by harassment or name calling. Sometimes they are simply isolated and excluded from the group and its resources. Social acceptance is a cherished resource, and its withholding can be a cruelly effective means of keeping people in line. Popularity depends upon being in step with prevailing opinions and social practices. For example, researchers have documented that peer approval and fear of rejection is often the primary motivator behind the decision of youths to initiate cigarette smoking and alcohol consumption (Friedman, Lichtenstein, & Biglan, 1985; Hunter, Vizelberg, & Berenson, 1991).

Campus Popularity and Political Opinions

Theodore Newcomb (1943) was intrigued by the impact of campus climate on attitude change and interpersonal relations. His campus of interest was the newly created Bennington College in Vermont, where he was a faculty member. At that time Bennington had about 250 female students and 50 faculty members. Two features of Bennington and its students made Newcomb optimistic that he could learn something about social influence. First, although the faculty at Bennington was quite liberal, the student body tended overwhelmingly to come from conservative backgrounds. Second, the campus dynamic encouraged close contact between faculty and students and between upper and lower classes—for example, freshmen were integrated into living groups with upperclassmen. Newcomb hypothesized that students might be affected by the campus climate and become more liberal over time. He measured students' political attitudes by eliciting their attitudes toward issues such as business monopolies, unions, and income tax rates.

Newcomb found that three generations of Bennington students did indeed become more liberal during their time at Bennington. Most relevant to the present discussion, however, was his finding on the relation between political liberalness and popularity: The more liberal students became, the more popular they were with their peers. For example, the most liberal students tended to be the ones their peers regarded as "most worthy" to represent Bennington College in a national convention. On the other hand, those who remained conservative tended to be socially isolated and to be perceived by counselors as overly dependent on their parents. It is unclear whether or not students at Bennington were directly pressured to change their views toward the prevailing campus norm. What is clear is that their popularity depended upon it. As one student told Newcomb (1943), "It's very simple, I was so anxious to be accepted that I accepted the political complexion of the community here. I just couldn't stand out against the crowd unless I had made many friends and had strong support" (p. 132).

Sorority Popularity and Eating Behavior

Almost 50 years after Newcomb's study at Bennington, Christian Crandall (1988) conducted another investigation of social influence on a university campus. His interest was the effect of social influence on the incidence of bulimia, an eating disorder in which individuals usually alternate periods of huge food consumption with purging, forcing themselves to throw up. There was much evidence that eating practices and body image were central to the lives of college women, and Crandall wanted to see if the tie between popularity and norm conformity was as strong here as it was in the case of political attitudes at Bennington half a century earlier.

Because his campus of interest was much larger—the University of Michigan—and because the relevant population was primarily women, Crandall focused on the relation of these variables within college sororities. Crandall's first study focused on a single sorority. He collected two measures from the women in this sorority. First, to identify friendship groups or cliques, he had the women list their 10 closest friends within the sorority. Second, he had the women complete the Binge Eating Scale (BES), which asked women questions about purging (either by vomiting or restrictive dieting), the emotional consequences of binging for them, the extent to which they engaged in inconspicuous eating during a binge, and so forth. On the basis of their answers to these questions, he categorized the women as high, low, or moderate in their binging tendencies. Women with low BES scores reported that they were able to stop eating urges, did not feel that they had trouble controlling eating urges, and did not think a great deal about food. Women with high BES scores (most of whom fell short of clinical levels) reported frequent uncontrollable eating urges, indicated they spent a lot of time trying not to eat more food, and reported having days where they could not seem to think about anything else but food. Women with moderate BES scores fell between the two other groups, reporting, for example, a compulsion to eat "every so often."

Crandall found that cliques of women within the sororities did tend to cluster in the degree to which they binged—suggesting that disposition toward binging, for whatever reason, was an important factor in friendship formation. A second study that contrasted two sororities suggested why friendship cliques tended to be similar on this dimension. In this study, participants completed the friendship measure and BES measure both at the start of the academic year and again seven months later, when it was nearly over. In both sororities, a woman's score on a binge-eating scale was related to her popularity within the sorority. Interestingly, however, the pattern was different in the two sororities. In one sorority, popularity was associated with high BES scores. Friendship cliques that binged the most were the most popular and those that binged the least were the least popular. Moreover, within groups, those who binged the least were least liked and those who binged the most were the most liked. In the second sorority, the binging norm was less extreme. Here the most popular members were those intermediate in their binging. In both sororities, thus, popularity was tied to the group's conception of the appropriate degree of binging—though that norm differed across groups.

Conformity Without Pressure

We have seen that deviance from opinion or behavioral norms can have significant social costs. Groups do not like members who deviate from the norms of the group—and they show it. Sometimes the cost of deviance is measured in material or physical terms; other times it is primarily social or psychological. One of the most interesting findings to emerge from social psychological investigations of conformity is the power of social isolation: People intensely dislike being isolated from others (Baumeister & Leary, 1995). People's aversion to social isolation can even dominate their concern with their physical well-being. For example, one of the strongest predictors of unsafe sex among gay men is fear of making a negative impression (Gold, Skinner, Grant, & Plummer, 1991). That is, homosexuals (as well as heterosexuals; see Bryan, Aiken, and West, 1999) are actually prepared to endanger themselves in order not to violate norms concerning the preference for (and implied superiority of) unprotected sex.

Implicit Peer Pressure

Sometimes conformity occurs without any explicit pressure. People conform in the face of a more implicit pressure: that which arises simply from their desire to be accepted by their peers. Adolescents, for example, often smoke not because their peers explicitly pressure them to smoke but because they crave acceptance and believe (perhaps correctly) that by smoking they will be more acceptable. The implicit nature of this pressure is evident from the fact that best friends have no greater influence on smoking initiation than do non-friends in the social environment (Kandel, 1980). In either group, the higher the prevalence of smoking, the more likely a student is to begin smoking. Many adolescents apparently assume that if they want to be accepted, or at least seen as being cool–even by people with little other influence on their lives—they must take up smoking.

Explicit fear of punishment or estrangement, then, is not necessary for conformity to others—this is the crux of a famous series of experiments by Solomon Asch (1955, 1956).

The Asch Studies

Imagine you are participating in your first psychology experiment, which the experimenter tells you is concerned with "visual perception." You are a little nervous, but the task seems simple enough. You and six other participants are seated around a circular table and shown a card with a vertical line. With this line still in view, all the group members look at another card, which has three vertical lines of different lengths. One of these lines is the same length as the line of the first card; the other lines are perceptibly different in length. You and the other participants have to state your choice of the matching line aloud, one at a time. Your position at the table makes you the next-to-last person to respond. On the first and second trials, everyone ahead of you gives the response that you think is correct. Seems easy enough. When the third pair of cards is held up, though, everything changes. The five participants before you (who are really confederates of the experimenter) give a response that seems incorrect to you. Now it is your turn; what do you do? Do you stick to your convictions, remain independent, and give the correct response? Or do you conform to the group, giving the answer that you know to be wrong? Most participants confronted with this situation, devised by Asch (1955, 1956), go along with the incorrect majority on at least some of the trials.

Why do people conform in the Asch situation? It is certainly not fear of punishment or harassment. They have no reason to think that the other participants want them to conform, nor are they likely to fear exclusion or unpopularity—the others are strangers with whom they will not have a continuing relationship. Thus, none of the conditions that applied to Schachter's experimental situation applies here. Nor are we speaking of groups in which the cohesiveness is as great as in the sororities studied by Crandall.

What, then, produces self-censorship in the Asch situation? Why do people not say what they know to be true? One possibility is that the mistaken majority actually persuades them that their responses are correct. People want to be correct and often adopt or internalize others' opinions because they think they are correct (Deutsch & Gerard, 1955). Groups influence individuals, then, not only by exerting pressure but by providing information about "reality" (Cialdini, 2001).

How do we determine whether people have accepted (internalized) the position of the group or if they are merely censoring their true opinion out of social fear? The primary means of making this determination is to contrast the degree of influence that is observed in public and private. If people show the same degree of influence in their private responses (i.e., responses that they do not think will be known to anyone else) as in their public responses, then it would appear that they have changed their perception and are not merely censoring it. A discrepancy between their private and public responses would suggest that self-censorship was involved. What are participants in the Asch situation doing, then? The evidence suggests that they are at least to some extent censoring their private beliefs. We know this because the degree of influence found in the Asch paradigm is less when participants write their responses down and do not show them to the others than when (as in the original procedure) they indicate their responses by raising their hand.

Nonetheless, we still must ask *why* participants conform. Let us see what participants themselves said. Many of those who did not go along with the confederates reported feeling "conspicuous" and "crazy" and like a "misfit," "sore thumb," "wet blanket," "silly fool," and so on. (Asch, 1956, p. 31). The message seems to be that even when isolation has no tangible costs—as in the Asch experiment—it can nevertheless be a very unpleasant state. Perhaps we have come to associate isolation with bad things–such as persecution, ridicule, or being disliked–and have learned to avoid it (or feel anxiety and discomfort in response to it) even when the costs are not obvious. As a result, we try to avoid isolation even when no persecution is possible and we do not care about the group. Simply being out of step is sufficient to make us uncomfortable.

Conforming to an Ideal Self

When people conform, it is not always to the behavior of particular others; sometimes it is to a more general ideal or standard. In laboratory experiments the relevant norm usually is the behavior of others—for example, people's recommendations concerning Johnny Rocco or their perceptions of line length. In the real world, however, the relevant norm is often a more general value or ideal that may or may not be reflected in the modal behavior of the group. A good Bennington student, for example, was someone who espoused a liberal ideology—not just someone who followed others. Once students decided that they aspired to the liberal student ideal, it was the ideal that they conformed to rather than the specific behaviors of others.

Conforming to a Gender Ideal

Males and females in all cultures must learn what is and is not appropriate behavior for their gender (Shweder, 1982). Gender norms function like other norms—you violate them and others will stigmatize or socially isolate you (Prentice & Carranza, 2004). For example, males who are passive and dependent (male inappropriate behavior) and females who are aggressive and competitive (female inappropriate behavior) are consistently rated lower in both popularity and psychological adjustment than their gender normconforming counterparts (Costrich, Feinstein, Kidder, Maracek, & Pascal, 1975).

Gender norms are often so thoroughly internalized that conformity to them requires little by way of self-censorship. For example, males who put on pants when they get up in the morning are conforming to a Western gender norm for dress but most will do so reflexively, neither experiencing nor inhibiting an impulse to wear a skirt. Many instances of conformity to gender norms do involve self-censorship, however.

Consider the tendency of men to eat more than women. One reason for this difference is obviously biological: Men tend on average to be larger than women. But that's not the whole story. There is also a social norm that specifies that women should eat less than men, and conforming to this norm frequently involves self-censorship, especially for women. Like women who violate any gender norms, those who violate the norm to "eat lightly" tend to be viewed as masculine and unfeminine, irrespective of their body shape (Chaiken & Pliner, 1987). One consequence is that when women wish to be seen as feminine, they may actually eat less than they want to. Indeed, Mori, Chaiken, and Pliner (1987) speculated that women's food consumption, because of the eat-lightly norm, often is governed as much by what they think is a gender-appropriate portion size as by their appetite.

Mori and her colleagues tested their speculation in an interesting set of experiments that involved both male and female college students, though we only concern ourselves here with the females. Participants were told that the focus of the study was the impact of hunger on visual perception and that they should not eat for at least four hours before coming to the experiment. Upon arrival, participants learned that the experiment had a "hungry condition" and a "full condition" and that they had been assigned randomly to the latter condition. Having been assigned to the "full condition," the participant's first task was to eat enough of a small meal provided (crackers with various toppings) to become "comfortably full."

Joining the female participant during the eating phase was another participant (actually a confederate of the experimenter). In the condition of most relevance here, the confederate was male. Before meeting the confederate, participants had the opportunity to read a brief "profile" crafted to make him appear either "desirable" or "undesirable." In the "desirable condition," he was described as "interested in traveling, photography, athletics, and reading, and as planning to go to law school, and as currently 'unattached.'" In the undesirable condition, he was described as "having no hobbies or interests other than TV, parties, and reading *National Lampoon*, as having no career goals other than making money and as currently 'attached.'"

Mori and her colleagues predicted that the female participants, despite being hungry, would conform to the women-should-eat-lightly norm when they were in the presence of the desirable male—someone whom they presumably wanted to find them desirable. The results supported the prediction: The female participants consumed an average of approximately 9 crackers in front of the "desirable" male confederate as compared to 12 and a half in front of the "undesirable" male confederate. What makes the women's censoring of their food cravings in front of the desirable male especially impressive is that in so doing their own behavior actually deviated from, rather than conformed to, the male's behavior because he himself always ate 15 crackers. It may be true that one of the surest ways to make someone like you is to present yourself as similar to that person (Cialdini, 2001), but this was not the strategy pursued here. Rather than conforming to the behavior of the desirable male—and satisfying their hunger to boot—the females in this experiment instead conformed to the feminine ideal.

Conforming to a Pro-Environment Ideal

One of the interesting things about norms of conduct, even those that we embrace, is that they are not always salient to us. We often simply aren't mindful of the norms that apply to the situations in which we find ourselves. Others play an important role in reminding us of the norms that should be guiding our behavior. Sometimes they do this explicitly, as when parents and teachers remind (constantly, it often seems) young children of norms of conduct. Sometimes the actions of others by themselves are enough to remind us of a relevant norm, as an interesting set of studies conducted by Cialdini, Reno, and Kallgren (1991) reveal.

The norm of interest in these studies was that discouraging littering. Anti-littering norms (and laws) have strengthened considerably in recent decades, though littering still occurs. One reason people continue to violate this norm is that they don't embrace it—littering isn't something they feel is bad or at least so bad that it warrants accepting the inconvenience its avoidance requires. But Cialdini and his colleagues point out that another reason that this norm continues to be violated is that even people who support it do not always think of it at the time they experience the impulse to litter.

To test their speculation, Cialdini, Reno, and Kallgren (1991) decided to examine the effects of drawing people's attention to an anti-littering norm on their tendency to litter. Their study was set in an outdoor parking lot that the researchers had either cleaned up or had cluttered (with cigarette butts, paper cups, candy wrappers, etc.). The participants were people who had parked their car in the lot. As participants reached their cars, they found a "Please Drive Safely" handbill tucked under the driver's side windshield wiper; the experimenters had put one on all the other cars as well. The researchers were interested in what participants did with this paper. Would they throw the handbill on the ground, or would they take it into the car with them and dispose of it later? It turned out that whether the parking lot was littered or not didn't matter—in both cases, slightly more than a third of the participants tossed the handbill on the ground.

What did affect the participants' behavior was which of two actions an experimental confederate took as he passed the participants on the way to their cars. In one case, the confederate threw an empty fast-food restaurant bag he was carrying on the ground in front of the participant. In a second case, the confederate bent over and picked up an empty fast-food bag that was presumably dropped by someone else.

The results were interesting. Witnessing a confederate pick up litter reduced littering by participants dramatically (by about 80%) whether the parking lot was clean or not. You might be surprised that the confederate's anti-littering behavior suppressed people's inclination to litter even when the appearance of the ground suggested that littering was the norm. The likely reason for this is that the confederate's behavior reminded people of what they *should* do even if it was not what most people did do.

The most interesting result occurred in the condition where the confederate dropped the bag. Here the state of the parking lot did matter. When the parking lot was filled with litter, witnessing one more act of littering by the confederate, not surprisingly, had little effect on the behavior of participants—about a third of them still littered. On the other hand, witnessing the confederate litter in the clean parking lot *reduced* the participants' own inclination to litter by over 60%.

This outcome seems puzzling. Why would people be less likely to litter a clean parking lot when they had seen another person litter it than when they had not? This certainly is not a simple case of people's conforming to the behavior of another—if this were the case, those witnessing a littering confederate would have been more, not less, likely to litter. Rather, what the participants appeared to be conforming to was the anti-littering norm that the confederate's irresponsible behavior made salient to them. Just as seeing another behave in an outrageous manner can remind one of politeness norms, seeing another abuse the environment appears to remind some people at least of pro-environment norms. Having been reminded of the norm, they acted in accordance with it.

Conformity Without Awareness

Much conformity, as we have seen, occurs with full awareness on the conformist's part. Recall the women in Mori, Chaiken, and Pliner's (1987) experiment who conformed to the women-should-eat-lightly norm when they wished to impress their male partner. The fact that these women were also the most accurate reporters of the amount of food they consumed suggests that they were fully conscious of what they were doing. Such awareness is not inevitable, however, as conformity can and often does occur without awareness. One familiar example is the (sometimes embarrassing) mimicry of verbal and nonverbal behavior (think of yawning) that occurs in everyday interaction. We routinely mimic the gestures, expressions, and voice inflections of those we are interacting without any awareness that we are doing so (Chartrand & Bargh, 1999). Recall too Vorauer and Miller's (1997) study, described in Chapter 1, in which students were shown to be unaware that they had presented their own college experiences as more negative than they were because of their desire to be in sync with another student.

Speaking Quietly in the Library

Everyone knows that people are meant to speak quietly in libraries. But when we conform to this norm, do we do so consciously or unconsciously? Undoubtedly, we sometimes intentionally and self-consciously lower our voices in libraries, but conformity to the library norm can also occur automatically, without awareness, as some clever research by Aarts and Dijksterhuis (2003) demonstrates.

This research showed that simply presenting people with cues that made them think of libraries actually induced them, unwittingly, to speak more quietly. Here's how this was accomplished. Participants came to the laboratory believing that they were going to perform various computer tasks for different experimenters. The first task was announced as the

"Picture Task" and required that participants briefly view a picture of a certain physical environment for 30 seconds and then answer questions about it. Some of the participants were additionally told that they would actually visit the environment later; others were not. The picture that participants were shown was either the interior design of a library or an empty platform at a railway station.

Next, in a supposedly completely separate experiment, participants performed a word pronunciation task that involved assessing the sound pressure level of their voice in decibels. Specifically, participants were instructed to read aloud into a microphone 10 words that were presented for two seconds on the computer screen. Allegedly this information would be helpful in designing new communication systems. Data of each spoken word were filed by the computer and converted into a decibel rating, representing a measure of voice intensity.

The question of interest was this: Would simply providing participants with a cue (i.e., a picture) that made them think of libraries be sufficient to get them to act in a library appropriate manner? The answer apparently is: Yes, it is. Those participants who had seen the picture of the library and expected to visit a library later spoke less loudly in the next experimental task than those participants who had seen the picture of the railway station. Interestingly, participants who saw the picture of a library but did not expect to soon be visiting one spoke no more quietly than those shown the picture of the railway station. Being reminded of situational norms, then, can induce us to censor our behavior, but only if we expect to soon be in those situations.

Summing Up

People's words and deeds often diverge from their personal inclinations and conform to those of others. Fear of material or physical punishment is one reason for this effect. Deviants are often severely punished. As this chapter shows, however, inclination to conform to social norms does not depend on fear of reprisal. People will conform, as they did in the Asch experiments, even when the social group consists of strangers who exert no explicit pressure and have no power over them. People do not like being out of step with others in their social environment. To avoid the discomfort of being out of step, people will act contrary even to deeply held convictions and their sensory experience. The dread of social isolation will sometimes induce people to change their thoughts and feelings, but more often it simply motivates them to censor their still retained thoughts and feelings in the presence of others who see things differently.

Chapter Review

1. Present evidence to support the claim that individuals who have deviant opinions are punished in psychology studies, in jury decision making, and in cabinet meetings. Describe how the empirical research and the case studies of real juries and cabinet meetings bear on this conclusion.
2. Present evidence to support the claim that behavioral deviants are punished in the classroom, the workplace, and the street corner.
3. Briefly describe the methods used by Newcomb and by Crandall in their studies on popularity and violation of group norms. In addition, describe their conclusions about the relationship between popularity and being in step with norms.
4. Examine Asch's famous research on conformity.
    a. Describe the methods he used.
    b. Describe his key findings.
    c. Explain why participants conformed in his experiment. Describe how their reasons for conforming were different or similar to the reasons given by participants in the studies by Newcomb; Crandall; Mori, Chaiken, & Pliner; and Cialdini, Reno, and Kallgren.
5. Lay out the logic of conformity when one is trying to act similar to an ideal self. How does this type of conformity differ from conformity in which one follows the behavior of others? Use Cialdini, Reno, and Kallgren's research to describe the two types of norms.
6. Describe the role of awareness and attention in conformity. Present research from this chapter and earlier chapters that suggests that at times (a) people are aware of their conforming behavior, and at times (b) people are not aware that they are conforming. Additionally, describe research suggesting that people are most likely to conform when norms are made salient.

Going Beyond the Chapter

1. In reading Newcomb's and Crandall's research, you may have wondered how people know what the norm is and how researchers know how to predict what the norm will be that individuals are striving to conform to. For instance, Bennington students became more liberal to match the political attitudes of the faculty at their college. It is possible, however, that Newcomb's participants could have been more influenced by the attitudes of their peers, which were quite conservative. Similarly, Crandall found that in the two sororities he studied, different types of eating behavior

(high binging in one, intermediate binging in the others) predicted popularity. Develop a framework for predicting what the norm will be. What factors seem important to include in this framework?

2. The discussion at the beginning of the book suggests that, given the high value placed on freedom and individuality in our culture, many think that self-censorship is inherently bad; inherently, however, it may not be either good or bad. Present your opinion about whether conformity is (a) inherently bad, or (b) neither good or bad. Do you think that the conception of conformity's goodness varies across cultures? Do you think that the level of conformity people demonstrate varies across cultures? If so, which cultures do you think would display the most and least conformity? Why?

3. In Asch's research, participants seemed to conform because they felt uncomfortable being out of step. They did not actually begin to see the longer lines as the same as the shorter lines. They just said what others said because they did not want to appear and feel different than other people. This may be a key reason that individuals conform. Yet while reading about this research, you may have wondered about other situations in which people actually do change their opinions to be the same as others. Consider under what situations you believe that individuals would not be self-censoring their behavior but instead would be changing their behavior to be the same as that of others because they now believed that the others' behavior was correct. Consider whether the following factors might influence this change of opinion: the ambiguity of the task they are doing, the novelty of the task, and the strength of their private beliefs.

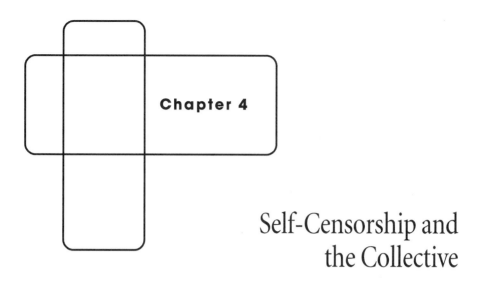

Chapter 4

Self-Censorship and the Collective

The stresses and strains of urban living were a hot topic in the late 1960s, a circumstance on which Bibb Latané and John Darley (1968) capitalized in staging one of the best-known studies in social psychology. The participants were Columbia University undergraduates in New York City—a favorite laboratory for the study of urban life. The students were recruited for what they were told would be an interview on their perceptions of the difficulty of living in the city. Upon their arrival, participants were escorted to a room where they were asked to sit and complete a lengthy "urban living" questionnaire. The experimenter meanwhile left "to do some work" in an office down the hall. The purpose of the study actually had nothing to do with the students' thoughts about urban living. Its real purpose was to see how they reacted to an event that occurred as they completed the questionnaire.

Soon after participants began working on the questionnaire, the experimenter introduced smoke into the room through a small vent in the wall. For the entire experimental period or until the participants took action, smoke continued to flow into the room in irregular puffs. By the end of 4 minutes, enough smoke had filtered into the room to obscure vision, produce a mildly acrid odor, and interfere with breathing. There were two conditions in this experiment: In one condition, participants were alone in the room; in a second condition, participants were in three-person groups. The typical participant in the individual (alone) condition behaved in a very reasonable manner. Half reported the smoke within 2 minutes of first noticing it, and three-quarters in this condition reported the smoke within four minutes of its introduction. Nothing puzzling here. But consider the group condition. Given that 75% of participants reported the smoke when alone, we might expect a very high percentage of the three-person groups to include at least one reporter. In fact, in only three of eight groups (38%) in this condition did even one participant report the smoke. Moreover, of the 24 people run in these eight groups, only one person reported the smoke within the first 4 minutes and only three people reported the smoke before the experimental period ended.

This experiment, often referred to as "the smoke-filled room" study, is one of a number by Latané and Darley (1970) that demonstrate a counterintuitive finding: the likelihood that bystanders will intervene in an emergency situation decreases as the number of potential helpers increases. Darley and Latané offer two explanations for this puzzling finding. The first focuses on the concept of *diffusion of responsibility*. According to this account, as the number of bystanders increases, the responsibility any one of them feels to act decreases. This hypothesis offers a plausible explanation for the inaction observed in many emergency situations but not for the inaction observed in the smoke-filled room experiment. It strains credulity to think that participants in the group condition of this experiment were reluctant to take action because of a diminished sense of responsibility for the would-be victims—the latter, after all, were the participants themselves.

A more plausible explanation for people's inaction in the smoke-filled room study is the second account that Latané and Darley proposed—that bystanders are less likely to define a situation as an emergency the more numerous they are. But why are bystanders less likely to define a situation as an emergency when they are part of a group than when they are alone? Conventional wisdom has it that two heads are better than one, so why wouldn't emergencies be more often recognized for what they are when more heads, eyes, and ears are present? The answer lies in a phenomenon known as *pluralistic ignorance* (Allport, 1924).

Pluralistic Ignorance: When Individual Fear of Overreaction Leads to Collective Underreaction

Consider the circumstance of people who confront a situation that appears potentially dangerous, either for themselves or for someone else. To begin with, the situation is likely to make them confused, uncertain, and anxious. If they are alone, individuals feeling this way are likely to take action—usually either by approaching the source of the danger or by fleeing from it. If they are with others, however, these individuals will have an additional concern: the impact that taking action will have on the impression that others form of them. If the situation constitutes a real emergency, others likely will think well of anyone who takes action, possibly even thinking he or she is a hero. But what if it is not a real emergency? For example, what if the smoke isn't what it looks like? In these cases, anyone who takes action, far from being viewed as a hero, is likely to be viewed as a busybody, an alarmist, or simply a nut.

Because of the potential costs of overreaction, it makes sense that people in situations like that created by Darley and Latané first try to gauge the degree of alarm or confusion in others while being careful not to betray their own confusion and distress. Latané and Darley (1970) describe the predicament of bystanders as follows:

> No member of a crowd wants to be the first to fly off the handle, the one to cry 'wolf' when no wolf may really be present. Too great a show of concern may itself be embarrassing, and it also may prematurely commit the bystander to a course of action he has not had a chance to think through. Until he decides what to do, each member of a crowd, however truly concerned he may be about the plight of a victim, may try to maintain a calm demeanor, an unruffled front. (p. 40)

Bystanders' façades can be so convincing that everyone concludes that there is nothing to be concerned about. In the words of Latané and Darley, "Looking at the apparent impassivity and lack of reaction of the others, each individual is led to believe that nothing really is wrong" (p. 41).

In the postexperimental interview, Darley and Latané probed participants for the thought processes by which they came to convince themselves that "nothing unusual" was going on. Many thought the smoke was either steam or air-conditioning vapors; several thought it was smog, purposely introduced to simulate an urban environment; and two (from different groups) actually suggested that the smoke was "truth gas" filtered into the room to induce them to answer the questionnaire accurately. Participants might well have continued to think that something was not quite right–but apparently much less so after seeing the reactions of the others.

The dynamic wherein people act similarly to one another but conclude that they feel or think differently is called *pluralistic ignorance* (Miller & McFarland, 1987). In essence, pluralistic ignorance occurs when the group (plurality) is ignorant of itself. In the case of bystanders to an emergency, for example, no group member is certain about whether there is an emergency, but each group member is certain that every other group member is certain (that it is not an emergency).

Basically, pluralistic ignorance involves three steps:

Step 1. People censor their true feelings or thoughts for fear of embarrassing themselves or being socially rejected by others.

Step 2. People falsely conclude that others are expressing their true feelings and thoughts, even though they too are self-censoring.

Step 3. People conclude that their own feelings and thoughts are not shared by others.

Pluralistic Ignorance and Group Decision Making

Pluralistic ignorance is not confined to groups consisting of strangers thrown together by happenstance, as in most emergency situations. It occurs in formally constituted decision-making groups as well. The dynamic in these cases typically takes the following form: Someone presents a proposal or urges a course of action with which the other group members disagree. Fearing that they might find themselves in the uncomfortable position of being the odd person out, the dissenters do not immediately voice their objection but try first to determine where the other group members stand. During this intelligence-gathering phase, group members censor their own concerns and feelings so as not to betray these possibly deviant reactions to the others. In doing this, group members act like so many (unwitting) confederates in communicating something they do not really believe. By mistaking one another's failure to express concerns as evidence that they have no such concerns, group members come to question the validity of their own, convincing themselves that their opinions are unfounded—or at least not shared by others.

The Origins of Pluralistic Ignorance: The Illusion of Transparency

Perhaps the most puzzling step in the three-step process just described is the second step. Why do people assume that the behavior of others is more genuine than their own? Why do they not infer that others' support for the emerging consensus, despite appearances, is likely no stronger than their own? Two perceptual biases working in tandem or independently are likely responsible. The first is that people fail to recognize how convincing their façades are, mistakenly thinking that their inner alarm must be registering at least somewhat in their public appearance. Not recognizing how well they have concealed their ambivalence and uncertainty, they take the public nonchalance of other bystanders as reflecting a genuine inner calm.

The second bias at work is people's mistaken assumption that they are more concerned with appearing foolish or naïve than are others (McFarland &

Miller, 1990). If bystanders do not recognize that the motive that induced them to dissemble has as powerful an influence over others, they will not recognize that the identical behavior of themselves and the others has the same significance. Knowing that it is the fear of looking foolish that leads them to look outwardly calm, they nevertheless think something else must be responsible for the public nonchalance of others—namely, their belief that there is nothing to be alarmed about.

People's belief that they have communicated their true feelings more clearly than they have has been termed the *illusion of transparency* (Miller & McFarland, 1991). There are two reasons that people tend to overestimate the transparency of their true feelings or beliefs. First, people think that their true feelings leak out in their public behavior more than is actually the case. People believe that even if they wished to, they would be unable to conceal any strong emotion (e.g., fear) from others (Gilovich, Savitsky, & Medvec, 1998). Second, people have an inflated view of their skill at communicating their private thoughts: They think that their subtle attempts to communicate their true feelings are more successful than they are (Vorauer, 2001). In summary, whether they think they have done so intentionally or not, people tend to believe that they have communicated their private thoughts and feelings more clearly than they have.

The Illusion of Transparency Among Bystanders to an Emergency

Bystanders to emergencies succumb to the illusion of transparency when they fail to realize how well they have concealed their confusion and uncertainty behind their cool, unruffled outward appearance. Thinking that their alarm over the potential emergency is more evident than it is, bystanders conclude that the others—who exhibit comparably few signs of alarm—are genuinely much less concerned about the situation than they are. In other words, failing to recognize that they look as untroubled as the others, bystanders fail to realize that the others are actually as troubled as they themselves are.

Gilovich et al. (1998) conducted an experiment that cleverly demonstrates the role that the illusion of transparency plays in the reluctance of bystanders to intervene. The predicament confronting the (three naïve) participants in this experiment was whether or not to report a fourth participant (confederate) who violated an experimental rule. The infraction involved helping another participant to solve problems while the experimenter was out of the room, despite the experimenter's parting warning that "if for any reason your performance level is not an accurate indication of the effort and ability you bring to the task, then the experiment will be a failure and the data will be useless to us" (p. 341). Participants were thus confronted with a dilemma analogous to that encountered in real-life emergencies: Should they intervene (and save the threatened experiment) or not? As predicted, participants did not intervene to stop the confederate, with the exception of two participants who engaged in minimal forms of intervention (e.g., "Are you supposed to be giving us hints?").

According to the experimenter's cover story, the study was ostensibly concerned with the impact of a group's working environment on its productivity. Upon his return, the experimenter administered a lengthy questionnaire that both fit the cover story and probed the real questions of interest—that is, (1) whether anyone had violated the rules of the experiment, and if so, who; (2) how concerned they were about this individual's behavior, as well as how concerned they believed they appeared to others; and (3) how concerned each of the other group members appeared to be.

The results revealed clear evidence of pluralistic ignorance: Participants indicated that they were more troubled by the rule violation than were the other similarly passive participants. The results also revealed clear evidence of an illusion of transparency: Participants estimated that they had appeared more troubled to others than they had. Thinking that the others did not look as troubled as they themselves felt, participants apparently concluded that the others were not as troubled.

Pluralistic Ignorance and the Perpetuation of Unpopular Social Practices

Pluralistic ignorance arises not only in isolated novel situations like emergencies; it also arises in everyday situations with ongoing consequences. One such consequence is the perpetuation of group practices that few if any members of the group support.

The Perpetuation of College Drinking Practices

In the 1990s, alcohol use by college undergraduates was a major concern of university administrators and public health officials across the country. Surveys showed that even though the use of other recreational drugs had dropped significantly, alcohol use was declining much more slowly (Berkowitz & Perkins, 1986).

In explaining this phenomenon, authorities commonly point to peer influence and social norms. It is well established that peers powerfully influence the drinking behavior of students and that drinking is central to the social identity and social life of many college students (Perkins, 1985).

It is nonetheless puzzling why students appear so comfortable with drinking practices given how dangerous these practices often are. Even if the moderation-advocacy efforts of administrators and parents leave students unmoved, why are the students not moved by their ample personal experience with the problems caused by drinking? Within their first few months at college, students are exposed to vivid and irrefutable evidence of the negative consequences of excessive alcohol consumption: They nurse sick roommates, overlook inappropriate behavior and memory losses, and hear about serious injuries and even deaths that result from drinking. They may even have negative experiences with alcohol themselves and have noticed its effects on their academic performance. One might think that such accumulating evidence would leave most students at least somewhat, if not extremely, uncomfortable with campus drinking practices. It must not cause such discomfort, however— otherwise campus norms would surely change, wouldn't they? Not necessarily!

To the extent that pluralistic ignorance pervades campus drinking practices, it is quite possible that individual student attitudes may be disconnected from campus norms, with student attitudes being less pro-alcohol than campus norms. To begin with, even if students are themselves uncomfortable with drinking patterns, they will hesitate to express or act upon this discomfort if they are worried that their peers will disapprove of them. By concealing their own discomfort, however, they signal to others that they are comfortable— thereby reinforcing the pro-alcohol norm.

Considerable evidence now attests to the existence of pluralistic ignorance around alcohol consumption in colleges (Prentice & Miller, 1996; 1993). Perkins and Berkowitz (1986) asked students to select from among five statements the one that best represented their own feelings about drinking and the one that best represented "the general campus attitude toward drinking alcoholic beverages" (p. 964). Student responses showed that they had moderately tolerant attitudes toward alcohol. Sixty-five percent of the sample said they agreed with the statement, "An occasional 'drunk' is okay as long as it does not interfere with grades or responsibilities." Fewer than 20%, however, were willing to endorse either of the following more extreme statements: (1) "An occasional 'drunk' is okay, even if it does occasionally interfere with grades or responsibilities," and (2) "A frequent 'drunk' is okay, if that's what the individual wants to do." On the other hand, more than 60% selected one of these two more permissive statements as representing the general campus attitude toward drinking.

We now have an answer to the puzzle posed earlier. Permissive student drinking norms can persist without comparably permissive student attitudes as long as the students assume that their peers hold attitudes congruent with the prevailing norms. In Chapter 3 we saw the power that group norms can exert on social behavior; here we see how potent norms can be even when they are illusory. People will conform to what they *perceive* to be the group consensus even when pluralistic ignorance has rendered their perception wrong.

Pluralistic ignorance may keep unpopular norms in place, but how does it arise in the first place? How might students communicate that they are more comfortable with drinking behavior than they are? They are likely to do this through both their actions and their reactions to the actions of others. On one hand, they may drink more (and more often) than they would if they did not believe that this behavior was normative. They might also exaggerate the amount they drink and strive to convey a "rosy" picture of their drinking experiences. On the other hand, they might be reluctant to express either disapproval or alarm over the drinking excesses of others when they find themselves in the role of bystander. They may even join others in joking about the drinking exploits of others and in encouraging new and grander exploits in the future.

Note that this form of pluralistic ignorance is not explained simply by students' *appearing* more comfortable with drinking than they are—if they recognized the deceptive façades of their peers, as was true with the bystanders described earlier, there would be no pluralistic ignorance. This inference escapes them, at least in part, because of the illusion of transparency. Students believe their true feelings about drinking to be more obvious than they are—even to their friends and roommates. Prentice and Miller (1996) provided experimental evidence that the illusion of transparency contributes to pluralistic ignorance surrounding alcohol practices. These researchers recruited unacquainted female students to participate in focus groups to discuss various campus issues, including the role of alcohol in campus life. Following the discussion, each student completed a questionnaire in which she rated the comfort with alcohol of each of the other members of her discussion group; how comfortable the other members believed her to be; and how similar her opinions were to theirs.

The results revealed that the participants concluded that the other group members were more comfortable with alcohol than they themselves were. More interesting than the evidence of pluralistic ignorance, however, was the evidence of the transparency illusion. Participants assumed that the degree of comfort other participants attributed to them was both much lower than it was and much closer to their true comfort level than it was.

Failure to recognize the extent to which their public behavior masks their private feelings may not be the only factor contributing to students' mistaken sense of where they stand in relation to their peers. Even if students recognized that they appeared as comfortable as did their peers, they may still think that peers' public comfort is more genuine, less muted by self-censorship, than is their own. Despite knowing that they are only *acting* comfortable because they fear presenting themselves otherwise, students may nonetheless assume that their peers *act* comfortable because they *are* comfortable.

The Perpetuation of Group Conflict

Such errors in the perception of self and others have consequences not only for relationships between individuals but also for relationships between groups. Although intergroup differences make intergroup tension nearly inevitable, groups routinely exaggerate whatever real differences exist between their own group and other groups. That is, people tend to assume that members of other groups are more extreme in their behavior, attitudes, and ideologies than they are. This misperception occurs whether the groups represent different roles within a formal structure (e.g., prisoners vs. guards), different nationalities (e.g., Palestinians vs. Israelis), different lifestyles (smokers vs. nonsmokers), or different beliefs (pro-life advocates vs. pro-choice advocates). In all of these cases, group members tend to see the other side as more extreme and more homogeneous than they are (Miller & Ratner, 1998; Ross & Ward, 1996; Robinson, Keltner, Ward, & Ross, 1995; Toch & Klofas, 1984).

One relevant study focused on college students who acknowledged having either strong pro-choice or strong pro-life views regarding abortion rights (Robinson et al., 1995). Researchers presented these students with a series of questions about abortion (e.g., what kind of abortion scenarios are common vs. uncommon; what positive consequences and what negative consequences would be likely to follow from a tightening of abortion restrictions, etc.) and then asked them to give both their own responses to these questions and the responses they believed the average member of both their group and the opposing group would give. The results indicated that although the "pro-choice" and "pro-life" groups did differ in their responses, they did not differ nearly as much as members of the two groups assumed they did. It is easy to see how this bias could interfere with group relations. By underestimating their common ground, groups will miss many opportunities for cooperation and compromise.

In another error that further undermines both intergroup and intragroup harmony, people assume that the members of their own group are more extreme than they actually are. In the study just described, for example, partisans misperceived the extremity of both their fellow partisans and the opposing partisans. In effect, they experienced pluralistic ignorance: Holding moderate views themselves, people erroneously inferred that most members of their group held much more extreme views. In fact, pro-lifers actually saw their fellow pro-lifers as even more extreme than pro-choicers saw them. These ingroup and outgroup misperceptions likely derive from the same source: the adherence of partisans' public behavior to the sharply defined norms and positions of their social groups rather than to the less extreme positions of their private attitudes. Just as overestimating the extremism of the members of the other side can impede intergroup relations, so can overestimating the extremism of the members of one's own side (Prentice & Miller, 2002).

Ingroup (and outgroup) misperception (stereotyping, really) is especially problematic in social institutions. Prisons provide a well-studied example of such an institution. Study after study has shown that prisoners and guards misperceive not only one another but also members of their own group (Benaquisto & Freed, 1996). Guards believe that prisoners are more antisocial than they actually are; moreover, prisoners believe the same thing of each other. Similarly, prisoners believe that guards are less sympathetic to prisoners—and guards believe each other to be less sympathetic to prisoners—than the guards actually are. Toch and Klofas (1984) suggest that ingroup pluralistic ignorance and outgroup misperception both arise in these circumstances because pressure to defend the ingroup's values leads both prisoners and guards to act less sympathetically to the outgroup than their private views would dictate: "One knows oneself to be—or suspects oneself of being—tender minded, naïve, vulnerable, and prosocial. One evolves a tough façade to avoid being ridiculed. . . . Some of one's peers—a clear minority—are *truly* tough; others—like the person himself—are 'façade tough'" (p. 136).

When Attitude Change Occurs Without Norm Change

Pluralistic ignorance commonly arises when the attitudes of individual group members have changed. People who once held one belief but now hold another will be especially hesitant to speak their mind—either because they worry that their change of heart is not justified, or because they worry that it makes them seem gullible or unstable. Thus, a common consequence of pluralistic ignorance is that norm change often lags behind attitude change. For example, private attitudes and drinking norms on college campuses may have corresponded at one point but gradually separated, with the norms lagging behind—largely because of pluralistic ignorance. As we will see, social change requires not only that beliefs change but also that beliefs about the beliefs of others change.

The Perpetuation of Discrimination

One of the fruits of the civil rights movements of the 1960s and 1970s was the end of forced segregation between black and white Americans. This did not come easily, however. First, many whites were uncomfortable with the idea of desegregation. Perhaps more interestingly, however, many whites fell prey to pluralistic ignorance and failed to recognize that even as they became more comfortable with the idea of desegregation, so did their friends and neighbors. One of many national studies conducted in the late 1960s and early 1970s found that only 18% of whites favored segregation but as many as 47% believed that most did so. Thus segregation survived even after it lost majority support because people still believed it to have majority support (Fields & Schuman, 1976). Whether whites themselves held liberal or conservative racial views, they assumed that other whites held conservative views. Segregationists were thus more self-confident and emboldened—and desegregationists more self-doubting and timid—than was justified.

The history of sex discrimination likely followed a similar course. Because of pluralistic ignorance, the decision by all-male clubs to admit women was probably delayed, at least in some cases, much longer than the attitudes of the majority of males justified. Liberal and conservative males alike probably thought that the resistance to ending sex discrimination was greater among their peers than it was. This misperception likely led conservative males to be more vocal in support of the status quo and liberal males to be less vocal in support of change than they would have been if they had read their peers accurately.

The Perpetuation of Violence

Some years ago, two social psychologists, Richard Nisbett and Dov Cohen, became intrigued by a large regional difference in rates of violence in America. The South is by far the most violent region of the United States, with rates as high as three to four times that of the rest of the country. Nisbett and Cohen (1996) proposed that this difference reflects a *culture of honor* that exists in the

South. According to Nisbett and Cohen, strong norms for aggression developed out of the early economic and social conditions of the South—a frontier region long defined by a herding-based economy without much law enforcement. Under these precarious circumstances, men were socialized to protect their property, wealth, and families, and were expected to defend their honor with violence if necessary.

Nisbett and Cohen may be correct that economic circumstances explain the development of the culture of honor in the South, but how are we to explain its persistence in the present day when the conditions are so clearly different? One possibility is pluralistic ignorance (Vandello, Cohen, & Ransom, 2004). The persistence of norms of violence, like norms of discrimination, might result not from widespread actual support, but from a widespread misperception that others support such norms. In fact, research shows that southern white males do think others endorse "honorable" aggression to a greater extent than they actually do. In one laboratory study, Cohen et al. (1996) contrived to have southern and northern male college students bumped into and called "asshole" by a confederate. Southern males subsequently indicated that they expected observers of the event (and of their failure to retaliate) would rate them as less masculine (manly, courageous, tough, and so on). Their experience of being insulted did not change what southerners believed about themselves, however—only their estimate of what others thought of them. Insulted northern males, on the other hand, did not expect that others would think less of them for not responding to the antagonist.

In another study, Vandello and colleagues (2004) found more evidence that southern white males misperceive support for the culture of honor. They provided scenarios to southern and northern men such as the following: "Kevin is at a bar one evening. He is sitting at a table eating chicken wings and having a beer. Another guy walks by and spills beer all over Kevin's shirt and then walks on without apologizing. Kevin gets up and punches him." After the men had read the scenarios, Vandello et al. asked them "What is the chance (0–100) that you would have punched the provoker if you were in the same situation?" The responses of the southern and northern men were similar, with each group saying that there was roughly a 25% chance of their punching the person. The two groups did differ, however, in their responses to a second question: "Imagine a random sample of 100 male students at your university. How many of them (0–100) would have punched the provoker in the same situation?" Southern males predicted that many more of their peers would retaliate than did the northern males.

In summary, at least one reason honor-directed aggression remains prevalent in the South is that southern males believe it enjoys stronger support among their peers than it does. Whether the mistaken belief that others support a code of violence leads one to be more aggressive oneself or simply to be more tolerant of aggression in others, unwanted violence is likely to be perpetuated.

When Norm Change Occurs Without Attitude Change

Sometimes events change norms regarding behavioral practices without producing comparable changes in private attitudes. Revolutions are one such circumstance. For example, Alexis de Tocqueville (1955/1836) proposed that the private attitudes of the French toward the church in the mid-eighteenth century did not undergo nearly as abrupt a negative shift after the French Revolution as did the public support of the church. De Tocqueville's (1955/1836) account of this dynamic eloquently describes pluralistic ignorance at work: "Those who retained their belief in the doctrines of the church because of being alone in their allegiance and, dreading isolation more than error, professed to share the sentiments of the majority. So what in reality the opinion of only a part . . . of the nation came to be regarded as the will of all and for this reason seemed irresistible, even to those who had given this false appearance" (p. 155).

Klassen, Williams, and Levitt (1989) made a similar claim in their analysis of the so-called sexual revolution in the United States during the 1960s and 1970s. According to these researchers, people's attitudes during this period did not liberalize nearly as much or as quickly as suggested by their public pronouncements and the rhetoric of the ("free love") times. As during the French Revolution, however, the doctrine of the new "regime" tended to go unchallenged because of the mistaken assumption that it enjoyed the private support of the majority. Thus pluralistic ignorance seems to have accompanied (and possibly even aided and abetted) the sexual revolution.

Backlash

When new norms develop without widespread group support, there is always the possibility that the discovery of this fact will lead to a backlash against the norm and its supporters. This outcome frequently occurs after revolutions. The backlash against the so-called political correctness movement is another example. Consider white college students' attitudes toward affirmative action.

The politically correct position is to support affirmative action, but many white college students might not support it as strongly as their rhetoric suggests. To the extent that this is true, two things might happen. First, pluralistic ignorance might arise, with white students believing that, despite their public utterances, they actually are less supportive of affirmative action than are their peers. Second, if they discover that their opinions are not deviant and that they thus need not have toed the politically correct line or felt guilt over doing so, they might joyously participate in a backlash against the policy. The first of these possibilities has been documented (Van Boven, 2000); the second has not (yet).

Changing Attitudes Versus Dispelling Pluralistic Ignorance

We have seen the various collective consequences that individual self-censorship can produce. By concealing or censoring their true feelings for fear of isolation, people create conditions favorable to the emergence of pluralistic ignorance, which in turn can lead to conditions that few people (if any) would want. The perpetuation of unpopular social norms and intergroup tension are but two examples. An important implication of this analysis is that efforts to change attitudes, even if successful, may not suffice to change behavior unless the targets of persuasion also recognize that their peers' attitudes have changed as well. It is not simply individuals' attitudes that determine their behavior but also their perceptions of the attitudes of others.

This analysis suggests that the key to behavioral change lies in dispelling pluralistic ignorance, not simply in changing attitudes. Even if people may have been persuaded of the desirability of change, they will only be comfortable actually changing their behavior it if they think others feel similarly. A quasiexperimental demonstration of this fact was provided by America's experience with the prohibition of alcohol during the early part of the twentieth century. Although strongly advocated and enforced by various constituencies in America, prohibition never had majority support. Because people were reluctant to express their widely shared and growing anti-prohibition sentiment, however, it did seem to have public support (Robinson, 1932). This state of affairs changed with the advent of public opinion polls, which revealed the depth of anti-prohibition sentiment and thereby dispelled the national case of pluralistic ignorance. Prohibition, with its lack of majority support exposed, soon thereafter "collapsed like a punctured balloon" (Katz & Schanck, 1938, p. 175).

Vandello and Cohen (2004) speculate that a similar dynamic may have been responsible for the abrupt ending of the thousand-year-old practice of binding the feet of young girls in China. The fact that this practice, which resulted in the deformation of women's feet (to a length of generally around 3 inches), ended within a generation after families in various regions of China formed antifoot-binding societies suggests that the practice was sustained at least partly by widespread pluralistic ignorance. Presumably, the creation of these societies promoted awareness of the gap between people's private attitudes and their public behavior, thereby dispelling the pluralistic ignorance that kept the increasingly unpopular practice in place.

Schroeder and Prentice (1998) conducted a more controlled test of the effects of dispelling pluralistic ignorance in the context of alcohol use on campus. First-year college students were randomly assigned to participate in one of two types of hour-long discussion sessions about alcohol use during their first week on campus. The two types of sessions were identical except for the content of a 20-minute discussion segment. In the norm-focused condition the discussion centered on pluralistic ignorance and its implications. Students were presented with data showing pluralistic ignorance regarding alcohol use on campus and were encouraged to talk about how these misperceptions might have developed. They were also asked to reflect on how misperceiving the norm for drinking might affect social life on campus. In the individual-focused condition (following many existing programs designed to change drinking behavior), the discussion centered on how individual students can make responsible decisions about alcohol consumption. Students were encouraged to reflect on the types of situations in which they might encounter alcohol at the university, to explore their options in those situations, and to consider the personal and social consequences of various courses of action. Four to six months after the discussion, students in both conditions completed self-report measures of their alcohol consumption.

Did dispelling pluralistic ignorance reduce students' drinking behavior to a level more consistent with their attitudes? Apparently, it did: Students in the norm-focused condition reported consuming 40% fewer drinks each week than did students in the individual-focused condition. From their responses to additional measures collected during the initial and follow-up sessions, it appears that dispelling pluralistic ignorance produced a change in drinking behavior by making students aware of the variability of their peers' attitudes (see also Haines & Spear, 1996).

Summing Up

The false impression that people convey when they censor their thoughts and feelings affects not only how others see them but also how they and others see their common situation. People rely heavily on their perceptions of others when interpreting situations and deciding upon the appropriate actions to take in those situations. When group members self-censor, the resulting miscommunication—termed pluralistic ignorance—can have significant consequences for the group. For one thing, when group members conceal their anxieties about a situation (e.g., a potential emergency) from one another, their collective action often assumes that there is nothing to be anxious about. No one is certain about what is going on but, because everyone conceals his or her uncertainty from the others, everyone is certain that everyone else is certain that there is nothing to be anxious about. Pluralistic ignorance, born of self-censorship, can also lead to the perpetuation of circumstances that no one wants—for example, the perpetuation of unpopular social norms or unwanted intergroup conflict.

Dispelling pluralistic ignorance requires either that group members be induced to stop self-censoring or that they otherwise be made aware of their peers true feelings and beliefs. Changing people's personal attitudes will not always be sufficient to get them to change their behavior. When pluralistic ignorance exists, it will also be necessary to change their perceptions of the attitudes of others.

Chapter Review

1. Examine Latané & Darley's famous experiments on the bystander effect.
   a. Describe their research hypothesis in the "smoke-filled room" study.
   b. What were the experimental conditions they included to test their hypothesis?
   c. Describe their methods.
   d. Describe their key findings.
   e. Explain why participants responded as they did in the various conditions.
2. Define pluralistic ignorance, laying out its three key steps. Use one of the examples in the chapter or presented at the beginning of Chapter 1 to illustrate the phenomenon and its basic steps.
3. The second step of pluralistic ignorance seems puzzling. Draw on research presented in the chapter to provide at least two possible reasons that

individuals believe others' self-presentations even when they know that they themselves are not expressing their true selves.

4. Pluralistic ignorance may play out in a number of domains and serve to perpetuate social practices that are actually unpopular. Present the logic of how pluralistic ignorance may serve to perpetuate

    a. illusions about students' comfort with drinking.

    b. group conflict, using Robinson et al.'s research on pro-life and pro-choice college students as an example.

    c. race and gender discrimination.

    d. violent behavior in southern males.

5. Explain in terms of pluralistic ignorance the intriguing notion that attitudes (or norms) about a topic may change but corresponding norms (or attitudes) may not accompany this change.

6. Using information from this chapter, discuss the potential effectiveness of reducing the negative consequences of one of the unpopular social practices described in question 4 by (a) changing individuals' attitudes, and by (b) dispelling pluralistic ignorance. What are two ways that one could dispel pluralistic ignorance?

Going Beyond the Chapter

1. Chapter 2 examined situations in which medical staff members noticed problems of which the surgeon did not seem aware yet did not say anything for fear of jeopardizing the surgeon's public image. One solution that hospitals take to handle this problem is to have many staff members in the operating room. Using what you have learned in the first four chapters of this book, how would you make the hospital operating room safer? Would you recommend having many staff members in the operating room? Consider not only the role of social etiquette and the power of the surgeon's definition of the situation in his or her operating room but also the effects of diffusion of responsibility.

2. This chapter highlighted the role of pluralistic ignorance and self-censorship in influencing individuals' behavior in emergency situations. Darley and Latané, however, additionally emphasize the role of diffusion of responsibility. In the chapter, we argue that diffusion of responsibility is an incomplete explanation for participants' behavior when they themselves could be harmed by not acting. However, while reading the text, you may have wondered whether pluralistic ignorance was also an incomplete explanation for participants' behavior. Are there aspects of bystander nonintervention that cannot be explained by pluralistic ignorance? For

instance, imagine that you live in an apartment complex with five apartments and that late one night you hear someone screaming outside. Darley and Latané suggest that you would be more apt to help if you knew that no one was home in all of the other four apartments than if you knew that others were home. Why? Imagine that you could not tell how others were responding to the screaming but still were less likely to act when you knew that others were also witnesses. Can pluralistic ignorance account for this finding? How about diffusion of responsibility?

3. Prentice and Miller as well as Perkins and Berkowitz provide evidence that students believe that other students are more comfortable with drinking than they are. They suggest that this divergence between private attitudes and perceived norms is the result of pluralistic ignorance. As you were reading these results, however, you may have wondered whether the divergence may instead reflect the efforts of participants to present themselves as socially appropriate and their peers as less appropriate. Do you think that these social desirability concerns could explain their data? Why or why not? How could one determine the effects of social desirability on participants' responses?

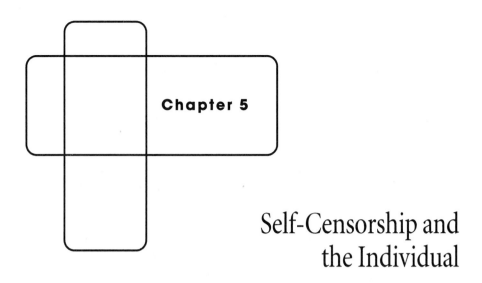

Chapter 5

Self-Censorship and the Individual

"**A** long time ago lived an emperor who above all liked beautiful clothes. . . ." Thus begins one of the most famous of Hans Christian Andersen's stories. One day, it continues, two con artists arrive in the empire. They pass themselves off as weavers and boast of knowing how to weave the most marvelous cloth imaginable. But clothes made from this cloth, they say, have the strange property of being invisible to fools. The emperor is delighted to hear this; now he will be able to rid his empire of all fools. He orders the two weavers to begin work but soon becomes impatient and dispatches two of his most faithful advisors to examine the weavers' progress. When the two con artists, who pretend to be very busy at their task, ask the advisers what they think of the cloth, the advisers, of course, see nothing. They do not admit this, however, but instead praise the work, as they do to the emperor when they report back to him. The emperor decides to go himself to see the famous cloth. When his two advisers extol the quality of the weavers' "work," the emperor realizes with great distress that he sees nothing. Still, he is careful not to admit this and requests that the weavers sew the cloth into a set of beautiful new clothes for him. He will display his costume, he decides, at a special ceremony attended by all his subjects. The great day arrives. The con artists dress the emperor in his marvelous clothes, "light as the web of a spider," they say. As the emperor's entourage moves through the town, everyone expresses admiration for the emperor's beautiful new clothes. The chorus of praise is broken by a single voice—that of a small child. Even though this voice is very quiet, it expresses what everyone thinks privately: "But he has no clothes at all!" This cry of innocence is repeated from one to another, first whispered and then amplified into an immense clamor and eventually an enormous burst of laughter as the people jeer at the deceit that has been perpetrated upon their ruler.

The emperor and his subjects were victimized twice: first by the con artists and second by pluralistic ignorance. Everyone pretended to see the new clothes because they did not want to look like a fool. So persuasive was their pretense, however, that everyone was convinced that everyone else actually saw the clothes. The emperor and his subjects revealed themselves as fools by their very efforts to prove that they were not fools.

This story demonstrates once again that pluralistic ignorance can have serious consequences for the group in which it arises. It also illustrates how pluralistic ignorance can yield serious consequences for the individuals who succumb to it. Despite the public praise they lavished on the clothes, the fact that they alone did not see the "beautiful" new clothes forced the private realization on each witness that he or she was a fool. The fraud perpetrated on the collective, once revealed, left the members of the collective feeling doubly like fools. The effects that pluralistic ignorance has on the self-regard, self-evaluations and feelings of the individuals experiencing pluralistic ignorance (as opposed to its effects on collective outcomes) are the focus of the present chapter.

Unwarranted Feelings of Inferiority and Inadequacy

When self-censorship gives rise to pluralistic ignorance, people will misperceive where they stand on various attitude, behavioral, and personality dimensions. This misperception can lead people to make inappropriately negative judgments about themselves.

Doubting One's Intelligence

One reason for the enduring popularity of the story of the emperor's new clothes is the commonness of the experience it captures—we have all been there. Consider the following all-too-familiar classroom dynamic: The professor pauses during a complex lecture to ask the students if they have any questions ("Do you all see my beautiful new clothes?"). At this point the bewildered but outwardly composed students furtively try to gauge their classmates' reactions. Despite widespread confusion, no hands are raised. This aspect of the dynamic is not particularly surprising—students can hardly be blamed for not wishing to embarrass themselves in front of their professor and peers. No one wants to look like a fool. The surprise comes with the next step in the sequence: Students misinterpret the silence and demeanor of the other students, inferring that their classmates understand the lecture and that they alone are confused. This misreading of the situation leaves students feeling inferior to their (seemingly less ignorant) peers.

Miller and McFarland (1987) conducted a study modeled after the classroom scenario just described. Participants were groups of three to eight undergraduates who were told when they arrived at the laboratory that the study's purpose was to investigate the layperson's theory of the self-concept, and they were to take part in a tape recorded discussion with one another later in the session. Supposedly for the purpose of preparing them for the discussion, participants were then asked to read an article describing various theoretical perspectives on the self. The article was written in a purposively difficult manner and was virtually incomprehensible to individuals without expertise in the area. The experimenter explained to participants that she would leave them alone to read the article while she did some work in her office.

Before leaving, the experimenter introduced the experimental manipulation. In one condition (the constrained condition), the experimenter explained as she left that "for purposes of experimental control" she could not answer any questions about the paper. In the other condition (the unconstrained condition), the experimenter indicated that participants could ask questions (although the procedure for doing so required that they risk embarrassing themselves). Participants were told if they "had any really serious problems understanding the article," they could stand up, leave the room, and approach her in her office several doors away. The experimenter then departed, leaving the participants to read the article. No participants in either condition sought out the experimenter during her absence.

When the experimenter returned, she asked the participants to complete a brief background information questionnaire before the group discussion. The supposed purpose of the questionnaire was to assess factors that might influence the course of the discussion. Three of these questions were designed to reveal any pluralistic ignorance experienced by the participants. They were: (a) "How well do you think you understand the article compared to the average other participant?" (b) "How much knowledge regarding the self-concept do you possess relative to the average other participant?" and (c) "How well do you think you would do relative to the average other participant if you had to write an essay on the topic of the self-concept?"

The results revealed clear evidence of pluralistic ignorance. Consider first the unconstrained condition, where participants were "free" to ask for help but presumably did not because of their fear of embarrassment. Miller and McFarland assumed that participants in this situation would interpret others' failure to seek help very differently from their own, and they appeared to do just that. They attributed their own failure to seek help to fear of embarrassment, whereas they assumed that the others did not seek help because they did not need it. The result of this misperception was that participants described themselves as much less knowledgeable and competent than their fellow participants. The very different pattern of results that emerged in the constrained condition supports this interpretation. Participants in this condition did not evaluate their own knowledge less favorably than that of their peers—presumably because they attributed both their own and others' inaction to the same source: the experimenter's prohibition against seeking help.

In summary, the price participants paid for not wishing to embarrass themselves was twofold: They missed out on some potentially valuable knowledge and they experienced a diminished assessment of their own knowledge and competence. Similarly, the pluralistic ignorance that emerges among students in classroom settings typically results in the perpetuation of both their actual ignorance (by preventing them from gaining clarification) and their illusory belief that they are more ignorant than their classmates. As with the emperor's subjects, the students' desire not to publicly reveal themselves as fools led them privately to see themselves as just this.

Doubting One's Competence

Self-censorship and the resulting pluralistic ignorance can leave people doubting more than just their intelligence—it can leave them doubting their competence more generally. A good example of this phenomenon is provided by Christine Maslach (1982) in her analysis of burnout in health care professionals. According to Maslach, pluralistic ignorance is common among members of this group because of their tendency to hide feelings of distress and anxiety behind an "I'm doing fine" mask. This widely maintained façade of control and composure leads people to assume erroneously that they are alone in their distress, a conclusion that only makes them more distressed. "It looks like they all know what they're doing, but I don't," they think. One of the former nurses Maslach interviewed describes this process eloquently:

> While we were in training, we were always being told to "be professional." No one ever said exactly what "professional" meant, or how to be that way, but I guess we all figured out that it meant being cool, calm, objective— and not being easily rattled by things. But I did get rattled and upset at times—like the first time a patient died. And I would be feeling panicky and angry and sad, but I would be fighting any expressions of those feelings because I knew they were not professional. Everyone else seemed to be handling things OK, which made me feel even worse—like a real failure

and a weakling who wasn't cut out for this kind of work. And I didn't dare say anything to them, for fear they would find out how weak I was and would think badly of me. It wasn't until much later that I discovered that they were just as scared and lonely as I was, and afraid that I would think badly of them. (pp. 11–12)

The experience Maslach described is certainly not limited to nurses. People in all occupations and roles are concerned with presenting themselves as competent at their job. Moreover, the competence that people wish to project extends beyond the specific skills that define their particular job or profession (e.g., nurse, teacher, policeman). Job occupants also want to appear to have the qualities of a competent group member. As Maslach noted, the nurses she studied wished to be seen as professional nurses and not as "sore thumbs," "weak links," or "sob sisters." In essence, they wished to stay clear of a label that would wound them psychologically—as it would any member of a group, work based or otherwise.

The types of behavior that prompts negative labels such as "wimp" or "brown noser" may be different in the locker room, the war room, the shop floor, the college dormitory, and the corporate boardroom, but the resulting stigma is the same. For this reason, people will often censor impulses to express negative feelings for fear that they will be diminished in the eyes of others. Too often the consequence of this self-censorship is that people end up diminished in their own eyes.

Doubting One's Virtue

At the societal level, the motives for acting in accord with the collective good do not matter much. Whether people pay taxes, donate to charity, or respond to a military draft out of fear or out of some nobler motive, society is equally well served. How individuals feel about their contributions to the public good, however, depends on their motivations for doing so as well as on the motivations they attribute to similarly acting others. If people think that their motives were purer than those of others, then they will feel virtuous; if they think that their motives were less pure than those of others, they will feel less noble–possibly even fraudulent. People have a formidable arsenal of psychological tricks to bolster their sense of general superiority (see Kunda, 1999), so concluding that they are less virtuous than others may be an infrequent occurrence. It does happen, however, and when it does pluralistic ignorance is often responsible, as a field study by Monin and Norton (2003) demonstrates.

The impetus for this study was a water shortage that occurred in parts of the northeastern United States in the aftermath of tropical storm Floyd in

September 1999. In the midst of broad appeals to limit water usage, Princeton University asked its students to refrain from showering for three days. Self-reports indicated that the majority of students honored this request–at least they reported taking fewer showers than they usually did. As you no doubt can imagine, refraining from showering was something many students found difficult to do. So why did they do it—why did they voluntarily walk around feeling grungy for three days? One possibility is that their feelings of moral obligation to their community motivated their shower abstinence. Another, less noble possibility is that their concern that their roommates and peers would disapprove of them motivated them. Of course, even if fear of embarrassment motivated students' socially responsible behavior, it is unlikely they would publicly admit this—it is much more likely that they would publicly profess community solidarity. As such, this situation is one that is ripe for pluralistic ignorance.

Pluralistic ignorance is just what Monin and Norton found when they asked the students how much they and their fellow students cared about the community. Those socially responsible students who refrained from showering actually thought that others who acted likewise did so for nobler reasons—at least they said that the others cared more about the community than they did. It appears that even though they knew that their motives were not entirely high minded, they assumed that the others' motives were. They did the right thing, for whatever reason but because of pluralistic ignorance did not get to feel as good about their actions as they should have.

Feeling Out of Step with Life Transitions

Sometimes pluralistic ignorance arises around transitions in life and development (Prentice & Miller, 1996). Consider the changes in the way that males and females react to one another at different developmental stages. At one stage of development (say, between the ages of 8 and 12), being a "normal" boy or girl requires that you have no interest in the other sex—indeed, that your attitudes toward them border on revulsion. During this stage boys and girls who, appearances to the contrary, don't hate the opposite sex as much as their group's norms demand may start to worry what this "perversity" says about them. Some years later (say, around ages 12–14), males and females find themselves subject to the opposite pressure: Now "normal" boys and girls are expected to be very interested in members of the opposite sex, including being sexually interested in them. Once again, those adolescents who don't feel comfortable with what they think their peers view as the appropriate relation to the opposite sex, regardless of how they present themselves to peers, will start to worry what their "deviance" says about them.

Two other examples of life transitions for which our culture provides clear "feeling" prescriptions are retirement and motherhood. Men and women are meant to feel happy and fulfilled in retirement. People who don't find themselves having these feelings, despite pretending to have them, can be expected to worry that something is wrong with them. In extreme cases, this can result in depression. The postpartum depression that many new mothers experience, for example, can be exacerbated by their erroneous belief that their joy in motherhood is not as strong or unwavering as is other mothers' (Eyer, 1996).

In the cases of retirement and new motherhood, people feel distressed because they feel less happy than cultural scripts and their (mistaken) sense of others suggest that they should feel. In other cases, people's distress derives from what they feel to be deviant feelings of *happiness*. The empty nest phenomenon provides an example. Cultural scripts lead people to expect that they will feel empty, sad, and restless when their children leave home. Many parents feel just the opposite, however, though they may publicly conceal these feelings so as not to appear to be unloving parents. Privately, they may worry what their true feelings suggest about the kind of parent and person they really are.

Unwarranted Feelings of Difference and Alienation

Pluralistic ignorance can leave people not only with unwarranted feelings of inferiority and inadequacy, but also with unwarranted feelings of alienation from their peers. The perception that they are out of step with their peers (whether or not it leaves them feeling inferior or inadequate) can leave people feeling less close to their peers as well as less committed to the identity they share. Alienation of this type is especially likely when the pluralistic ignorance pertains to attitudes and behavioral practices.

The Illusion of Universality

Feelings of difference and alienation emerge from a feature of pluralistic ignorance that we have not discussed thus far: the perceived relation of one's peers to one another. Pluralistic ignorance is characterized both by the mistaken perception that you differ from the average other and by the mistaken perception that your peers are more similar to one another than they are. This latter phenomenon is known as the *illusion of universality* (Allport, 1924). Any negative feelings engendered by people's belief that they deviate from the *average* of their peer group are likely to be compounded if they also hold the perception that their peers are highly similar to one another. Consider the psychological predicaments of two students: The first believes that students vary greatly in how comfortable they are with drinking practices on her campus and that she falls toward the uncomfortable end of the continuum; the second believes that all other students except her are comfortable with drinking practices. Both students believe that they are more uncomfortable than their peers, but the latter student, by falling prey to the illusion of universality, can be expected to feel much greater alienation from her peers than the former student does. In summary, feelings of alienation and deviance are especially intense when people misperceive not only their relative standing on some dimension, but also the similarity of their peers to one another on this dimension.

Prentice and Miller (1993) reported a study of college students' attitudes toward campus drinking practices that demonstrates the illusion of universality and its relation to unwarranted feelings of alienation. The study focused on Princeton students' reactions to the unilateral decision by their university's president to ban kegs of beer from campus. Princeton's president saw what came to be known as the "keg ban" as a largely symbolic act designed to demonstrate the university's concern about drinking on campus. The policy was enormously unpopular: Editorials appeared in the student newspaper, there was protest from alumni groups (who would no longer be allowed to have kegs at reunions), and even the other administrators at Princeton distanced themselves from the president's policy. But despite the public outcry, private sentiments were not nearly so negative toward the keg ban. It was a time of great concern about alcohol use on campus, and many students privately expressed approval that the president of the university was willing to take action on the issue. Also, the ban was only on kegs, so students (and alumni) would still be free to drink bottled beer and other forms of alcohol if they wished. In reality the keg ban was not that big a deal, despite outward signs of outrage.

Shortly after the ban was instituted, Prentice and Miller asked 94 Princeton students to indicate how they felt about the university's new policy banning kegs on campus, and, in comparison, how the average Princeton undergraduate felt about the keg ban. Attitudes were fairly negative toward the keg ban but, as Prentice and Miller expected, students thought that the average student held an attitude even more negative than their own. About three-quarters of the surveyed students indicated that the average student felt either much more or somewhat more negatively than they did about the keg ban. Almost all of the remaining students said that the average student felt about the same as they did, and only 3 of 94 students said that the average student felt somewhat more positively than they did. Prentice and Miller also asked students several questions about their willingness to take public action related to the keg ban and about their identification with the university in general. First, students were asked to indicate how many signatures they would be willing to collect in protest of the ban and how much of their time they would be willing to spend discussing ways to protest the ban. Then they were asked what percentage of reunions they expected to attend after graduation and how likely they were to donate money to Princeton after graduation.

Prentice and Miller expected that students who believed that they were deviants—75% of the students in the sample—would be less likely to take action on the keg ban and less connected to the university. In other words, they expected perceived deviance to be associated with distancing or disidentification from the issue and from the group—and that's exactly what they found. The further students believed they deviated from the norm, irrespective of their actual deviation, the less willing they were to collect signatures protesting the ban and the less likely they predicted they would be to attend reunions and to donate money to Princeton following graduation. Thus, when people feel out of step with what they think is a likeminded peer group, they are not only less likely to act on their convictions, but they also withdraw from the group, both physically and psychologically.

Feeling Both Superior and Alienated

It is important to note that pluralistic ignorance can leave people feeling alienated from their peers even if it does not leave them feeling inferior or inadequate. Alienation depends on the perception that one is out of step with a group of people who are in step with one another; it does not depend on feeling inferior to those others. Indeed, people can feel alienated from their peers and superior to them at the same time.

In fact, it is often difficult to tell whether perceptions of difference between oneself and one's peers yield a positive or negative self-evaluation. In the classroom scenario and in Miller and McFarland's (1987) experiment, it does seem clear that the emergence of pluralistic ignorance left people feeling badly about themselves. But in many other cases of pluralistic ignorance, the situation is much less clear. Consider college students' belief that they are less comfortable with campus drinking practices than their peers are: Will this belief leave them feeling positively or negatively about themselves? Quite possibly, different students will have different reactions. Some may feel that their moderateness says something good about them and others that it says something bad about them. Whichever the case, however, people's perception that they differ from their peers and that their peers are highly similar to one another results in alienation.

A similar situation arises around people's perceptions of their sexual attitudes and practices in comparison to those of their peers. Various studies indicate that people's beliefs about sexual attitudes and practices are characterized by pluralistic ignorance (Cohen & Shotland, 1996; O'Gorman, 1986). Sometimes people see themselves as more liberal in this respect; for example, people believe that they are more tolerant of pornography than is the average member of their community (Linz et al., 1991). Sometimes people see themselves as more conservative—for example, believing that they are less comfortable with one-night stands ("hooking up") than are their college peers (Lambert et al., 2003). But does seeing oneself as more sexually liberal (or more sexually conservative) than one's peers leave one feeling good or bad about oneself? Again, different people may feel differently. On one hand, believing that they are more sexually liberal may leave some people feeling liberated and enlightened and others feeling guilty and immoral. On the other hand, believing that they are more sexually conservative may leave some people feeling moral and responsible and others prudish and naïve. Whatever its effects on their self-regard, however, pluralistic ignorance surrounding sexual attitudes will likely leave its victims feeling less connected to one another. Whether people believe they are the only virgin or the only nonvirgin in their peer group, they are likely to feel distant from those peers, irrespective of how they feel about virginity.

In brief, even when people do not feel uncomfortable with the manner in which they differ from their peers, they may feel uncomfortable about the fact that they differ. Specifically, they will feel less close to their peers as well as less connected to the group identity they share.

Secondary Feelings of Deviance

Feelings of deviance result both from people's perceptions of difference between themselves and others (primary deviance) and from people's evaluations of their reactions to this difference (secondary deviance). Seeing oneself as different from others often implies that one should act differently from others; not doing so will often leave one feeling badly about oneself. Secondary feelings of deviance take many forms, though in all cases they derive from the perception that one lacks the courage to be true to one's private beliefs or experience. In the classroom scenario described earlier, feelings of negative secondary deviance actually compound the negative feelings of primary deviance. These students experience a double whammy of sorts: They must confront not only the fact they are more ignorant than their peers, but also the fact that they are too insecure to take action (i.e., raising their hand) to remedy this situation.

One common form of secondary deviance occurs when people compromise their true beliefs or perceptions and publicly conform to those expressed by others. Asch (1956) noted, for example, that many of the participants in his conformity experiments (see Chapter 3) felt badly for "bowing to pressure." By conforming rather than standing their ground, participants had to face the fact that they lacked the courage to tell it like they saw it. This is the common fate of those members of decision-making groups who find themselves going along with a decision with which they disagree (see Chapter 3).

In other situations, people experiencing pluralistic ignorance may feel guilty about betraying a deeply held value. Feeling that they are more moral or virtuous than others will provide little comfort to people if they feel they lack the courage to act on their superior values. Such a situation often arises in cases marked by prejudice and discrimination. Consider the case of a group of females in the presence of a high-status male who makes sexist comments. The females, even if angered by these comments, may wish to avoid a scene for reasons we discussed in Chapter 2. Concealment of their anger may induce pluralistic ignorance, however, leaving each of the women thinking that she alone was offended by the man's remarks. The self-recriminations that attend the feeling that she should have confronted the man might negate any (erroneous) feelings of superiority that she derives from thinking that she is more enlightened than are the other women.

A similar dynamic commonly occurs in race relations. Whites who feel they are more liberal on racial matters than their white peers often experience a profound sense of guilt if they do not act upon their conviction, which negates any superiority conferred by their sense of high-mindedness. Similar reactions may be experienced by blacks who feel that even though they may be more aware of acts of discrimination than their peers, they are cowards for not acting upon that heightened awareness. The cost of self-censorship thus includes feelings of guilt and self-recrimination along with feelings of alienation, inferiority, and inadequacy.

Behavioral Consequences for the Self

The consequences of pluralistic ignorance for individuals go beyond their feelings about themselves and their relation to their group. Pluralistic ignorance also affects people's actions and, as a consequence, their life circumstances.

Health-Endangering Behavior

Consider again the case of college students' perceptions of campus drinking norms. As previously discussed, misperceiving the norm can have psychological consequences for students—they can feel out of step with their peers and generally badly about themselves. Misperceiving the norm can also have practical consequences for the students, because they may end up drinking more than they want to or than is good for them. Or consider the finding that college students believe that their peers are more sexually liberal than they are (Cohen & Shotland, 1996): In addition to the effect this erroneous belief has on the psychological state of students, it can also lead them to take actions that they and their partners are uncomfortable taking. In one relevant study, gay males' reluctance to use condoms was shown to be partly the result of pluralistic ignorance: They mistakenly believed that other gay males did not share their comfort with condoms (Gold et al., 1991). Unwanted or unsafe sex is by no means the only health-endangering consequence that can result from pluralistic ignorance. It appears, for example, that female anorexia is fostered by women's perception that their peers value thinness more than they do (Sanderson et al., 2002).

Relationship-Impeding Behavior

The decision about whether to "make the first move" in initiating or deepening a social relationship is one many people find difficult to make. The reason, of course, is that none of us like to be rejected or embarrassed. As a compromise, many people in this situation try to subtly feel out the other person while being careful not to betray their own interest in case it isn't reciprocated. The problem, of course, is that by acting cool and aloof they signal to the other person that they aren't romantically interested in him or her. Thus can two people who are attracted to one another come to conclude that the other is not.

Coyness by itself, however, is not the problem. The interaction could still end happily if the two individuals realized that the other person likely feels as they do, despite appearances. Two people who both want to go through a door but hesitate to go first usually quickly resolve this impasse because they recognize that the other feels the same way. But this is not always the case in romantic situations. Instead, despite recognizing that they are acting cool and distant because of fear of rejection, people often think that the object of their romantic interest is not approaching them because he or she does not find them attractive. Unfortunately, the victims of this mutual situational misreading are the participants themselves.

Vorauer and Ratner (1996) conducted a series of studies to investigate this process. Their first study sought to establish that fear of embarrassment is a common impediment to people's approaching one another. These investigators asked college students a simple question: "Has fear of rejection ever been a significant obstacle to your pursuing a romantic relationship?" As Vorauer and Ratner expected, a large majority (over 75%) of college students responded affirmatively to the question. Indeed, 54% of students indicated that such a fear had completely prevented them from pursuing a relationship on at least one occasion.

Next, Vorauer and Ratner (1996) sought to determine if students thought that this type of inhibition affected them more than it did others. They did this by presenting students with the following scenario:

> Imagine the following situation. You are at a party; currently, you are not seriously romantically involved with anyone. Early in the evening, you are introduced to a single person who could be a potential romantic partner. You learn from a brief conversation that you have a lot in common. In your opinion, the two of you are equally attractive. Toward the end of the evening, you find yourself alone in the kitchen with the person. You talk with each other for a while. (p. 491)

Participants were then asked to make two separate judgments:

(a) Assume that you have become romantically interested in this person. How likely is it that a fear of being rejected would inhibit you from explicitly expressing your romantic interest to the person, or indicating that you would like to see him/her again?

(b) Assume that this person has become romantically interested in you. How likely is it that a fear of being rejected would inhibit this person from explicitly expressing their romantic interest in you, or indicating that he/she would like to see you again? (p. 491)

As expected, students thought that fear of embarrassment was more likely to inhibit them from acting than it would the other person. People know when fear of embarrassment is preventing them from taking action, but it is difficult for them to recognize its influence on such seemingly unfazed and indifferent others.

In a final study, Vorauer and Ratner (1996) appended the following ending to the scenario just described: "Neither of you explicitly expresses a romantic interest in the other, or an interest in seeing the other again. You head back to join the group in the living room" (p. 492). Then they asked the students what they thought was the most likely reason for their own inaction and for that of the other in the scenario. Consistent with the claim that interactions of this type are characterized by pluralistic ignorance, most of the students believed that their action would reflect a fear of being rejected and that the other's action would reflect their lack of interest in them.

We saw earlier that pluralistic ignorance can lead people to ignore the well-being of another, such as in bystander situations. We see here that it can also lead them to ignore, or at least undermine, their own well-being. How often do relationships go unrealized because people experience pluralistic ignorance and fail to recognize that the inaction of an attractive other reflects his or her fear of rejection rather a lack of interest?

Finally, it should be noted that the pluralistic ignorance arising here, as in the other situations, can have more than one cause. Vorauer and Ratner's research shows that people are inclined to attribute the very same action, performed by themselves and by another person, to different sources: fear of rejection versus lack of interest. It may also be the case, however, that people in these situations suffer from the illusion of transparency. That is, people may hold the mistaken assumption that their behavior actually communicates their interest, which, combined with their inability to detect similar interest in the behavior of the other, leads them to conclude that the other does not feel similarly. In a more general sense, pluralistic ignorance, begot by self-censorship, serves to diminish the likelihood that social bonds of various forms will develop fully.

Conflict-Perpetuating Behavior

Pluralistic ignorance not only prevents people from realizing desired outcomes, it also leads them to realize undesired outcomes. One situation in which the latter effect occurs is a common type of bargaining situation known as the *prisoner's dilemma*. To illustrate, consider two competing small business owners who are offered the opportunity to invest in an expensive advertising campaign. Each individual is thus presented with two options: Option 1, buy the advertising; Option 2, do not buy the advertising. If both parties choose Option 2, a mutually beneficial outcome results—they both save money and neither loses their competitive position relative to the other. On the other hand, if one chooses Option 2 and the other chooses Option 1, the latter person has a great advantage over the former. If both parties choose Option 1, however, a mutually undesirable outcome will result—they will both be out of pocket a lot of money without gaining any advantage over their competitor.

In fact, it is fairly common for people to end up in just this situation. Why? One reason is the pluralistic ignorance that arises from the fact that the motivation behind choosing Option 1 is ambiguous. People could choose this option out of fear of being exploited by the other or out of a desire to exploit the other. Put differently, the response one should take to prevent exploitation by the other and the response one should take to achieve the exploitation of the other are the same: Buy the advertising. This ambiguity leads to pluralistic ignorance and spiraling conflict (e.g., more self-defeating competition) because people often choose a course of action analogous to buying the advertising out of fear of exploitation, but they assume that the other has chosen the same option out of their desire to exploit them.

The structure of this situation is very similar to that facing potential (but unacknowledged) romantic partners. In both cases, by opting for a safe course of action, the parties permit each other to attribute their motive to something undesirable (i.e., lack of romantic interest, the desire to exploit), which leads in one case to the failure of the relationship to develop and in the other case to the spiraling of conflict.

Overcoming Pluralistic Ignorance

There are two main ways to combat pluralistic ignorance and the ills it produces. The first involves getting people to overcome their urge to censor themselves. When people are more willing to express their true feelings, pluralistic ignorance is less likely to emerge. Sometimes this happens naturally over time as people become more open and communicative with one another. The passage of time does not mean that one will inevitably become more candid, however. For example, Prentice and Miller (1993) found that pluralistic ignorance surrounding alcohol norms was as great among last-semester college seniors as among first-semester college freshmen. Sanderson et al. (2002) found a similar stability in the pluralistic ignorance surrounding college women's attitudes toward thinness norms.

The second means of reducing pluralistic ignorance is dispelling it— informing people that others feel the same way as they do. This is one reason that go-betweens who point out to disputing parties the similarity of their goals and concerns can play such a major facilitative role in the reduction of conflict cycles (Deutsch, 1973). People can also learn that others share their private attitudes, feelings, or habits by reading published polls or surveys (Shamir & Shamir, 1997). We saw earlier that the era of prohibition in America swiftly ended once polls began to appear indicating how unpopular it was. Some campuses have attempted to dispel pluralistic ignorance by publicly displaying students' real attitudes toward campus drinking practices. Support groups routinely reassure people that their circumstances and their reactions to those circumstances are not as uncommon as they think they are. When people's distress results at least partly from their mistaken sense that their reaction is abnormal, this information can be very effective. One can even dispel pluralistic ignorance by educating people about the way it works. For example, Schroeder and Prentice (1998) were able to reduce drinking among college students by educating them about the process of pluralistic ignorance more generally, not just how about it relates to beliefs about alcohol use.

Summing Up

People often conceal from others thoughts and feelings they think might be deviant. Sometimes these thoughts and feelings are deviant, but frequently they are not. Nevertheless, people often fail to recognize that the similar behavior of others is also inauthentic. When this happens, people are said to be experiencing pluralistic ignorance. In addition to its consequences for the collective (described in Chapter 4), pluralistic ignorance has consequences for individuals. When self-censorship gives rise to pluralistic ignorance, people will believe that they are more extreme in their attitudes, feelings, or behaviors than they are. This misperception, in turn, can lead people to misperceive where they stand on various attitude, behavioral, and personality dimensions. It can also lead them to feel alienated from their fellow group members. It can even leave them feeling alienated from themselves by making them feel badly about their concealment of their true feelings or their failure to act upon them. Informing people of their similarity to others, or encouraging them to self-censor less, will reduce many of the psychological ill effects of illusory deviance.

Chapter Review

1. Explain how Hans Christian Andersen's tale of the emperor's new clothes illustrates the phenomenon of pluralistic ignorance. What were the consequences of pluralistic ignorance for the various characters in this story?
2. Examine Miller and McFarland's study on pluralistic ignorance in the classroom.
   a. Describe the methods they used.
   b. Describe their key findings.
   c. Explain why participants responded the ways that they did in the various conditions.
   d. What were the implications of participants' not asking questions?

3. This chapter argues that pluralistic ignorance has a variety of implications for individuals' beliefs about themselves. Present the logic for this assertion and the evidence that pluralistic ignorance may leave individuals
   a. doubting their competence.
   b. doubting their virtue.
   c. feeling as though they are out of step in life transitions.
4. Using Prentice and Miller's research as an example, define Allport's illusion of universality and then describe how this illusion may strengthen the impact of pluralistic ignorance on individuals' feelings of alienation.
5. Present evidence that pluralistic ignorance may have the following negative behavioral consequences for the self.
   a. increased health-risking behavior
   b. lower likelihood of pursuing a romantic relationship
6. Chapters 4 and 5 consider two main ways to combat pluralistic ignorance (see also question 6 for Chapter 4). Describe these two methods and use evidence from the present chapter to assess the effectiveness of each method in alleviating the negative consequences for the self.

Going Beyond the Chapter

1. Drawing on Miller and McFarland's research on pluralistic ignorance in the classroom, develop a set of strategies that professors and students could use to encourage students to ask questions when they are confused. What should professors say? What are ways that professors could prove to a student that he or she is not the only one who is confused? What are things that students could say to other students to encourage them to ask questions?
2. Brainstorm about the norms on your campus. What is the perception of the "typical student?" Do you think that students in reality are quite different from this typical student? In other words, what campus norms do you think are misperceived because of pluralistic ignorance? What norms do you think are more accurately perceived? What factors predict whether the perceptions are accurate or not?
3. This chapter provides several examples of life transitions (puberty, motherhood, retirement) in which individuals may feel that they need to conceal their private feelings because they are not what are expected. Propose research to determine whether individuals self-censor in these contexts and whether they do actually feel out of step in them. What methods would you use? What experimental conditions? What participants? What pattern of results would you expect to support the ideas in this chapter? What pattern of results would refute them?

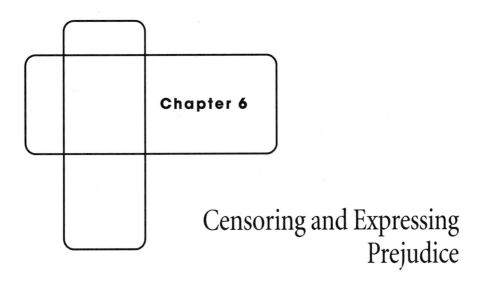

Chapter 6

Censoring and Expressing
Prejudice

"**W**ould you move if black people came to live in great numbers in your neighborhood?" In the 1960s almost 80% of white Americans answered "Yes" to this question. By 1980 less than 50% of whites so answered, and by 1997 the number had dropped to approximately 20%. Similar pro-black shifts have been documented in the positions whites express toward interracial marriage, school integration, and affirmative action (Schuman et al., 1997, 2002).

How are we to interpret white Americans' shifting responses to racial questions? The most optimistic interpretation is that anti-black prejudice among whites has receded almost to the point of disappearance. The least optimistic interpretation is that anti-black prejudice amongst whites remains as strong as ever, and only their willingness to honestly report their prejudice has actually changed. A third possibility, and the one endorsed by most social psychologists, is that the reduction in anti-black sentiment expressed by whites represents shifts in both their actual prejudice level and in their comfort in expressing their true feelings.

Consider the support black candidates receive from white voters as an example. The increasing number of elected black state and federal officials, even in predominantly white areas, reveals that whites are much more willing now than previously to vote for black candidates. Nevertheless, the number of whites who tell survey researchers they intend to vote for black candidates is consistently greater than the number of whites who actually cast their votes for black candidates (Clymer, 1989, 12 November; Finkel et al., 1991). Apparently, whites' desire to appear progressive on racial matters has outpaced their actual progressiveness, although some change has undoubtedly occurred here as well.

This chapter addresses the psychology involved in revealing and concealing prejudice. There are many disputes among experts on prejudice, but on one thing they all agree: The pressure not to appear prejudiced, especially racially prejudiced, has dramatically increased in mainstream America as well as in many other parts of the world. In contemporary America, the stigma attached to the label "racist" approaches that reserved for wife beaters and rapists (Crandall, Eshleman, & O'Brien, 2002). With prejudice becoming increasingly unacceptable, both its experience and expression have come increasingly under the control of inhibitory processes. Indeed, one cannot understand prejudice without understanding the role that self-censorship plays in its experience and expression.

Norms Against Racial Prejudice

The form of prejudice we examine most closely is that of white Americans toward black Americans. The reason for this focus is partly that the vast majority of prejudice research has focused on this form of prejudice, and research on other forms of prejudice (e.g., homophobia and sexism) shows highly similar results (see Fiske, 1998; Nelson, 2002). It appears that prejudice is prejudice. That so much prejudice research focuses on white Americans' prejudiced feelings and actions toward black Americans also reflects the unique place race relations have played and continue to play in American life (Jones, 1997; Myrdal, 1944). Furthermore, the feelings of white Americans toward black Americans reveal more clearly than most forms of prejudice the ambivalence that often underlies prejudice (Gaertner & Dovidio, 1986; Katz et al., 1986). For example, most whites strongly believe that blacks deserve equal treatment yet continue to harbor negative feelings toward blacks. In the view of many social psychologists, contemporary white Americans find themselves not so much free of prejudice as struggling, consciously and unconsciously, with their still present, if diminished, anti-black feelings. In the words of Gordon Allport (1954), "The intellect says no, but the emotion lingers."

The precariously fragile nature of whites' control over their anti-black feelings is revealed in a study of Rogers and Prentice-Dunn (1981). The experimental procedure required white college students to administer (or at least believe they were administering) electric shocks to another student (confederate) as part of a learning experiment. Participants were seated in front of a shock apparatus and were told that a signal would appear when they were to administer a shock, the intensity and duration of which they were to determine.

For half the participants the confederate was white, and for the other half he was black. Participants actually delivered somewhat lower-intensity shocks to the black than the white confederate when the confederate acted in a pleasant and agreeable manner. But when the confederate insulted, and presumably angered, them (he was overheard to say that he worried that someone as "dumb" as the participant could use the apparatus correctly), participants delivered more pain to the black confederate than the white confederate. It would appear that the white students in this experiment harbored latent hostility toward blacks, a feeling that they kept in check when their interaction with the black confederate went smoothly but that surfaced when they became angry.

Censoring the Expression of Prejudice

With the growing unacceptability of racial prejudice, it is not surprising that whites are motivated to keep the negative feelings they have toward blacks concealed both from blacks and from other whites. Research on beliefs and practices in many domains of moral significance—ranging from church attendance (Hadaway, Marler, & Chaves, 1993) to sexual activity (Kinsey et al., 1948)—has documented that people's desire to boost their image in the eyes of others frequently affects what they report. Moreover, people's self-presentations vary across audiences because audiences vary in their opposition to prejudice as well as in what they might consider to be an indication of prejudice. For example, whites present their opinions about social policies (e.g., affirmative action) as more pro-black in front of a black audience than in front of a white audience (Fazio et al., 1995).

People's treatment of members of other races also depends upon the audience. When they are in front of an audience that they anticipate will be vigilant for signs of racial prejudice, whites treat blacks no differently, and sometimes even better, than they treat whites (Dutton, 1973; Gaertner & Dovidio, 1986; Lowery et al., 2001). White college students, for example, were found to be more likely to stop and help pick up some dropped pencils for a black confederate than for a white confederate (Dutton & Lake, 1973). The treatment that blacks receive from whites in nonface-to-face contexts is often much less egalitarian, however (Crosby et al., 1980). For example, whites were found to be less likely to assist a black than another white when the request was made of them on the telephone (Gaertner & Bickman, 1971).

In light of whites' discriminatory behavior toward blacks in anonymous situations, it seems unlikely that their nondiscriminatory treatment of them in face-to-face situations is entirely genuine. More likely, it is their desire not to appear racially prejudiced, rather than the absence of such prejudice, that is responsible for the positive treatment that whites extend to blacks in front of an audience. Even here, they presumably are disinclined to help blacks, either because they feel antipathy toward them or simply because they are uncomfortable interacting with them. In face-to-face situations, however, the fear of appearing prejudiced overrides people's true inclinations.

The Search for Prejudice: Trying to Outsmart the Censor

The fact that people are increasingly reluctant to admit to prejudice has stimulated social psychologists to be more creative in studying it. In their search for manifestations of prejudice that people either cannot conceal or do not closely monitor, researchers also have learned much about the nature and function of prejudice.

Subtle Measures of Prejudice

The questions that researchers ask to detect prejudice have changed. It is inconceivable that a contemporary researcher would ask someone to respond to statements such as "The Negro [sic] is by no means fit for social equality with the commonest White people" (Hinckley, 1932). No mainstream white American could be expected to agree with the "blacks-are-inferior" premise of this question, and most would be insulted by the implication that they might. Researchers have replaced so-called blatant measures of prejudice with more subtle measures. The reasoning behind using these latter measures is not only that whites won't admit to agreeing with blatantly prejudiced statements, but also they genuinely will not agree with them. Researchers use subtle measures, then, both because the expression of anti-black feeling among whites is subtle and because the feeling itself is subtle. Rather than seething feelings of hatred, whites experience more subtle feelings of "discomfort, uneasiness, disgust, and sometimes fear" in the presence of blacks (Gaertner & Dovidio, 1986, p. 62–63).

To illustrate the psychology behind so-called subtle measures of prejudice, contrast the following two agree/disagree statements: "Blacks should not have an equal chance with whites for jobs" and "Discrimination against blacks is no longer a problem in the United States" (McConahay, 1986). Although these questions both focus on the issue of racial discrimination, there is an important difference (Jones, 1997). The first question directly taps the respondent's belief about the principle of discrimination: Is it acceptable or not? The second question does not directly tap the respondent's belief about the principle but instead taps the respondent's knowledge or perception of "fact." Has the principle of racial equality been achieved or not? Clearly, agreeing to the first question makes you prejudiced, but what about agreeing to the second question? Surely, even a nonprejudiced person could believe that the "facts" suggest that discrimination is no longer a serious problem in America. True, but someone who agrees with many such statements is likely to be prejudiced—at least this is the assumption behind scales that employ such statements (e.g., Biernat & Crandall, 1999). The reason that scales composed of so-called subtle measures produce more variation in responses and hence are better able to differentiate respondents is that respondents do not perceive such questions as measuring prejudice. People are willing to agree with subtle expressions of prejudice because they do not think that doing so makes them prejudiced. This presumably is why whites answer subtle questions, in contrast to more explicitly racial questions, the same whether in front of a black or white interviewer (McConahay, 1986).

Nonverbal Measures of Prejudice

A second means of circumventing people's efforts to conceal their prejudices is to move away from verbal responses and focus instead on people's nonverbal behavior. People communicate feelings nonverbally as well as verbally, and feelings that are concealed in people's verbal behavior often leak into their nonverbal behavior (DePaulo & Friedman, 1998). Researchers have found this to be especially true of negative feelings toward others.

Facial Expressions   Facial expressions are one form of nonverbal behavior that reveal feelings that words and deeds do not. A technique known as facial electromyography (EMG) permits researchers to detect even the smallest variation in people's facial muscles, which in turn can be compared with variations in their affective states. Vanman et al. (1997) took advantage of EMG technology to study anti-black feelings in whites. These researchers presented their white participants with slides of white and black individuals and asked them to imagine interacting with the people shown in the slides. The researchers also asked participants how friendly the people appeared and how much they thought they would like them. Participants' verbal reports communicated greater liking for the black person than for the white person, but their facial muscles told a different story. Analysis of their facial muscle activity revealed that when black faces appeared, white participants tended to show more activity in frowning than in smiling muscles—the opposite of which was the case when white faces appeared.

Voice Quality   Voice quality is another cue to emotional feeling that has been used in the search for evidence of prejudice. In one demonstrative study, Weitz (1972) invited white male undergraduates to participate in an experiment on "environmental effects on skilled behavior." The procedure required participants to converse over an intercom with someone who they thought was either a black or white fellow participant (actually a confederate). Weitz recorded participants' intercom conversations (primarily involving the participants' reading instructions to the confederate) and then had coders rate the voices for warmth and other affective qualities. As expected, the results showed that white participants revealed more negativity in their voices when they thought the person they were speaking to was black than when they thought he was white. Further strengthening the claim that participants' voice quality was a more reliable guide to their true feelings, the voice measure predicted the length of time they were willing to work with him in the future *better* than did their reported liking for the confederate. More interesting still, participants who were most positive toward the black confederate in their postconversation questionnaire responses also revealed the most negativity in their voices when speaking to him. It would appear that participants who experienced the most anti-black affect were the ones who most vigorously tried to deny it—possibly to themselves as well as to the experimenter. They could not control what they felt, but they could control what they *said* they felt.

Implicit Measures of Prejudice

By employing nonverbal and other nonreactive measures, researchers have been more successful in finding evidence of anti-black affect among whites than they have with more explicit (reactive) measures. More important, however, they have also learned more about the nature of prejudice. A set of prejudice measures known as implicit measures has been especially valuable in this regard (Greenwald & Banaji, 1995). *Implicit measures* are designed to assess the associations people have to different social groups—associations that they might not be willing to express openly or even know that they have (hence the term *implicit*). Thus implicit measures are designed to get behind people's defenses—under their radar, so to speak—and reveal their uncensored (especially negative) thoughts about different social groups.

The Theory Behind Implicit Measures   Before describing implicit measures and what they have revealed about prejudice, a brief digression into theory is in order. One way to think about prejudice is that it involves the association of certain feelings or thoughts (e.g., hostility) with certain social categories (e.g., blacks). Viewed this way, it follows that anything that makes one think of a social category should also make one think of the traits and feelings that one associates with that social category. This assumption constitutes the basis of what is known as the *spreading activation theory* (SAT) of memory (Collins & Loftus, 1975). According to SAT, when particular concepts or words (e.g., doctor) are activated (primed) in people's minds, associated words (e.g., nurse) are also activated. Psychologists use the term *activation* to refer to the extent to which words or concepts are available for cognitive processing tasks (e.g., word recognition).

Spreading activation can be demonstrated through a range of different measures (see Blair, 2002). One such measure is the *sequential priming task*. In this task, the speed with which people can identify words presented on a computer screen following the activation of a category (e.g., doctor) is taken as the degree of implicit association the person sees between the former and the latter. The well-established finding in this paradigm is that words associated with a recently activated (primed) word can be identified faster than unassociated words. For example, people can identify *nurse, blood,* and *hospital* as words (as opposed to non-words) faster following the presentation of the word *doctor* than after the presentation of an unrelated word like *tree* (Meyer & Schvaneveldt, 1971). A second measure known as the *word completion task* presents people with word fragments such as *bl—d* and asks them to convert these fragments into real words. This measure reveals spreading activation by showing that people tend to convert fragments into words that are associated with words that have been previously activated. For example, people for whom the word *doctor* has been primed are more likely to complete *bl—d* as *blood* than as *blond*.

Social psychologists interested in prejudice soon recognized that SAT and the methods used to investigate it could be valuable tools in their quest to detect what more explicit measures could not. Specifically, researchers should be able to find out what people think about a social category by seeing what thoughts they activate in response to cues associated with the category in question. Consider an example: Assume that we want to test the hypothesis that people feared doctors—perhaps we are interested in why people are reluctant to visit doctors. Assume further that our direct questioning of people about whether or not they feared doctors revealed no support for our hypothesis. How else might we test our hypothesis? Employing a sequential priming task of the type just described would be one possibility. That is, we could see if people were faster to recognize or identify fear-related words (e.g., *fearful, anxious, scared, nervous*) following the activation of the concept *doctor* than other concepts. If they did, this would suggest that people implicitly associate doctors with fear, irrespective of whether they admitted this or even were consciously aware of it. This experiment has not been done (as far as I know) because social psychologists are not much interested in people's implicit association with the category *doctor*. However, many experiments have been undertaken to determine the implicit associations that people have to different social categories, including those that whites have to the social category *blacks* (Greenwald & Banaji, 1995).

Evidence of Implicit Prejudice   A large number of studies using implicit measures of one type or another do find that whites implicitly associate blacks with negativity (Dovidio et al., 1997). In one illustrative study, Fazio and his colleagues reasoned that if whites experience an automatic negative reaction to African-Americans, then exposure to photographs of African-Americans should, in accordance with SAT, speed up the evaluation of negative words and slow down the evaluation of positive ones. To test this reasoning, these researchers showed white participants a series of 24 words–12 positive words (e.g., *attractive, wonderful*) and 12 negative words (e.g., *annoying, disgusting*)–on a computer screen. The words were shown for only 315 milliseconds (experienced as a flash of light). Participants' task was to indicate as fast as they could whether each word was good or bad by pressing one of two buttons ("good" button vs. "bad" button) connected to the computer presenting the words. The results were as predicted: White participants took longer to identify positive adjectives (i.e., press the "good" button) following the presentation of a black face than a white face. In contrast, they took less time to recognize negative adjectives (i.e., press the "bad" button) following the presentation of a black face than a white face.

And its not just negative words that whites are faster to recognize after exposure to black faces. Whites for whom the black stereotype has been activated by black primes (black faces presented on a computer screen too briefly to be recognized) are also faster to recognize crime-related objects, such as guns and knives (Eberhardt, Goff, Purdie, & Davies, 2004). They are also more likely to misclassify a tool as a weapon following exposure to black primes (Payne, 2001).

Whites' tendency to associate blacks with negative feelings and negative thoughts can even distort their reactions to individual blacks. Specifically, whites will be inclined to categorize or interpret an individual black's behavior negatively if the thoughts his or her racial cues activate tend to be negative.

Indeed, whites will judge the behavior of blacks more negatively than the identical behavior of whites (Duncan, 1976; Sagar & Schofield, 1980). Whites will even see another white as more aggressive following the activation of the black stereotype (Devine, 1989).

Social psychologists who employ implicit measures have been especially interested in two interrelated questions. The first of these concerns individual differences in implicit reactions. In particular, do all whites have the same associations to blacks, differing only in what they are willing to say about them, or are there differences among whites in implicit responses? The second question concerns the extent to which it is possible for people to control their implicit reactions, or at least their influence on their thoughts and actions, toward particular others.

Do People Differ in Implicit Prejudice?   The strength of the association between negative traits and blacks, as revealed by implicit measures, varies considerably among whites (Greenwald, McGhee, & Schwartz, 1998). This is significant because virtually all whites (and blacks) know the cultural stereotypes on which these associations are based and thus might be assumed to have the same associations (Devine, 1989). The question here is whether the observed variation in strength of implicit reactions relates to variation in intensity of prejudice. It appears that it does. For example, variation in participants' responses to Fazio et al.'s (1995) implicit measure was found to correlate with variation in their responses to two explicit measures of prejudice. One of the latter involved the ratings that a black female experimental assistant made of how friendly the white participants were to her. The more negative the white participants' implicit associations to black faces were, the less friendly the assistant judged the participants to be. In a similar study, McConnell and Leibold (2001) found that the more negative whites' implicit associations were to stereotypic black names (e.g., Jamal and Yolanda) as compared to stereotypic white names (e.g., Fred and Mary Ann), the more anxious and uncomfortable they were in the presence of a black experimenter.

Controlling Prejudiced Thought

The thrust of the research described thus far suggests that people can control their expression of prejudice, but only to a degree. They can control what they say and to some extent what they do, but they cannot control their thoughts or feelings. More recent work, however, suggests that people can even censor their prejudiced thoughts and feelings. We consider two forms of thought control: postconscious stereotype control and preconscious stereotype control.

Postconscious Stereotype Control

Research shows that group stereotypes can be activated in people's minds by a range of cues without their awareness. But is it inevitable that activated stereotypes will affect people's reactions to members of the stereotyped group? It appears not. People can control not only whether they publicly express a prejudiced belief but also whether they apply those beliefs in their interactions with individual members of the stereotyped group. However, preventing unbidden stereotype thoughts from influencing our judgments is not easy; it requires considerable cognitive effort. When people find themselves cognitively taxed (e.g., by distraction or tiredness), they will find it especially difficult to resist applying any activated thoughts that they are experiencing.

An interesting experiment by Galen Bodenhausen (1990) shows that for people to successfully suppress activated stereotypes, or at least undermine their impact on social perception, they need to have all their wits about them. Bodenhausen classified participants by their circadian arousal patterns, or biological rhythms, into two types: "morning people," who describe themselves as most alert in the morning, and "night people," who describe themselves as most alert at night. He then had them participate in an experiment at either eight in the morning or nine in the evening. The experimental procedure required participants to read about a court case and then decide on the guilt or innocence of the defendant. The researchers varied whether the defendant did or did not belong to a group that was stereotyped as likely to perform the crime under consideration (e.g., the defendant in an assault scenario was either Hispanic or white). As Bodenhausen predicted, morning people were more likely to find the stereotyped defendant guilty when tested at night and night people were more likely to find the stereotyped defendant guilty when tested in the morning. Other research shows that people are also more likely to use stereotypes when they are under the influence of alcohol than when they are sober (Von Hippel et al., 1995) and when they are angry than when they are calm (Bodenhausen, Shephard, & Kramer, 1994). In summary, if even those who are motivated to avoid prejudice are to successfully curtail the application of activated stereotypes, they must have sufficient cognitive resources to engage in the controlled, deliberative, and effortful thought that is required (Fazio & Towles-Schwen, 1999).

Preconscious Stereotype Control

Some psychologists claim that the nonprejudiced yet stereotype-aware individual may have even greater powers of self-censorship. These researchers argue that people can prevent themselves from activating stereotypes in the first place and not simply suppress them after they have been activated. People do this, the argument goes, by associating nonprejudicial rather than prejudicial thoughts with racial cues. After all, people are presumably not hard wired to associate cues of particular ethnic groups solely with negative or stereo-typed thoughts (Nelson, 2002).

In this spirit, Moskowitz et al. (1999) proposed that a strong motivation to be egalitarian should result in racial cues' activating egalitarian rather than stereotypic thoughts in a person. They tested their hypothesis in a complicated but interesting experiment. They began by searching for whites who could be characterized as having a strong goal to be egalitarian when dealing with other groups, especially blacks. They did this by first asking a large group of college students to "describe their current hopes and goals." On the basis of their responses, the researchers designated students "egalitarians" or "nonegalitarians." Two examples of goal statements made by students designated as egalitarian were (1) "to help created a world where equality and justice exist for all groups, where Whites and Blacks are treated equally under the law," and (2) "to work in the inner city so I can make sure that African-American children have the same opportunity and access to education that were available to me."

Two weeks after they had completed the life goals questionnaire, participants were brought into the laboratory, where they were exposed to computer-presented primes (presented at a subliminal rate of 200 milliseconds) of faces of either a white or a black person. The experimenters then presented participants with stereotype-relevant or stereotype-irrelevant words and asked them to pronounce them as quickly as possible. Moskowitz et al. found that nonegalitarians exposed to a black prime activated the cultural stereotype of blacks, as reflected by the fact that they were faster to pronounce stereotype-relevant than irrelevant words. Egalitarians in the black prime condition, however, did not pronounce stereotype-relevant words faster than stereotype-irrelevant words.

But if racial cues do not activate stereotypes in egalitarians, what (if anything) do they activate? A second experiment by Moskowitz et al. suggests an answer. This experiment revealed that following a black prime, egalitarians responded faster to egalitarian-relevant words (e.g., *equality, fairness, broadminded, tolerance,* and *justice*) than to egalitarian-irrelevant words. For some people, then, it appears that encountering a member of a stereotyped group does not automatically activate the stereotype of that group. For them, the same cues that produce stereotype activation in others produce the activation of egalitarian ideals and beliefs.

Even temporarily aroused egalitarian motivation may suffice to prevent the activation of stereotypes, as a study by Fein et al. (2002) revealed. Participants in this study first completed a questionnaire that, they were told, revealed them to be racist. White participants then read a newspaper article about a black or white lottery winner, after which they performed a word fragment completion task. Those who did not receive feedback suggesting that they were racist showed the customary activation of the black stereotype on this measure, but those whose racial impartiality had been questioned revealed no activation of the black stereotype. Presumably their redoubled desire to uphold their non-racist self-image enabled them to prevent the activation of the black stereotype. This worked whether the prime was subliminal or not.

Let us return to the question with which we began this chapter: What has changed about mainstream white Americans' feelings toward black Americans over time? First, the social norms against the expression of prejudice against blacks (as well as many other groups) are more powerful than ever; consequently, whites have become increasingly hesitant to express beliefs or feelings that could be interpreted as prejudiced. Second, the social definition of what constitutes prejudice has broadened. Many beliefs that would not have been labeled racist fifty years ago are so labeled today. These two changes, in turn, have produced further changes. Most important, whites' actual attitudes have become less anti-black over time. Fifty years ago, 80% of whites publicly agreed "There should be separate sections for Negroes on streetcars and buses" (Hyman & Sheatsley, 1956); today the vast majority of whites would not only publicly but also privately disagree with that statement. It is also true, however, that whites have become less willing to report those anti-black beliefs that they still do hold. For example, it is likely that a nontrivial number of the 80% of whites who today publicly disagree with the statement, "Over the past few years blacks have gotten more economically than they deserve" (Henry & Sears, 2002), do so only because they do not want to appear prejudiced.

The fact that people scrupulously censor their words and actions so as not to appear prejudiced has led researchers to adopt nonreactive measures of prejudice—most notably, implicit measures. The use of these measures has yielded bad news and good news. The bad news is the confirmation of the hunch that whites continue to harbor negative thoughts. The good news is the discovery that prejudiced thoughts or associations are not an automatic and inevitable consequence of exposure to a member of the target group. Under the right conditions, people can prevent themselves not only from applying those prejudiced thoughts that situational cues activate in them but possibly also from allowing such thoughts to be activated in the first place (Kunda & Sinclair, 1999).

Licensing Prejudice: Finding Acceptable Channels of Expression

We previously sketched the dilemma of people faced with the prospect of interacting with a member of a group about whom they have negative feelings. On one hand, they risk violating anti-prejudice norms and possibly their personal standards if they act upon their negative feelings. On the other hand, they risk compromising their actual beliefs and motivations if they refrain from acting upon their negative feelings. Our discussion thus far has focused on the circumstances under which people's response to this dilemma is to inhibit, at least publicly, the expression of negativity. We now turn to a consideration of the circumstances under which people respond to the dilemma by *expressing* their negativity. Our focus here is not those circumstances in which people find themselves unable to maintain control of their negativity—for example, because they are tired, anxious, or angry—but those in which they have found a way to express their negativity that does not violate egalitarian standards or norms.

Disguising Racial Bias in Innocent Attire

Most whites do not want to say or do anything that could be construed as reflecting anti-black prejudice. For some, this stems from a concern with their public image; for others, from a concern with their private image. In neither case does the fear preclude the expression of negativity toward blacks—only the expression of negativity that might be construed as racist. If the negativity could be attributed to something other than racism, its expression is much more likely.

Race-Neutral Explanations Research using a variety of paradigms shows that people's concern with appearing prejudiced will be allayed to the extent that their discriminatory behavior could be explained by something other than prejudice (Hodson, Dovidio, & Gaertner, 2002). One such study (Frey & Gaertner, 1986) examined white students' willingness to help a fellow student (black vs white) win bonus points toward a prize in a game of Scrabble. The experimenters manipulated the player's race as well as his worthiness of help. They manipulated "worthiness" by varying how hard the player was trying and whether the problems he encountered were of his own making. When the task had been unusually hard and the Scrabble player was having trouble through no fault of his own, white students helped the black player as much as they helped the white player. When the player got behind because of laziness, however, the white students helped the black student much less than his white counterpart. It would appear that the white students were disinclined to help the black student even in the "deserving" condition but overcame the urge to act on this impulse because they did not want to be (or appear) prejudiced. They were liberated to act upon their disinclination in the "undeserving" condition, however, because the motivation for not helping was ambiguous: It could reflect either prejudice or reluctance to reward laziness. Targets of prejudice are well aware of the dynamic captured in this experiment, which is why they strive so hard to avoid acting in ways that would license ill treatment by others who, without such justification, would censor their prejudiced impulses (Jones et al., 1984, Steele, 1997). The pressure on targets of prejudice to avoid providing justification for discrimination is all the greater because prejudiced individuals are disposed to make attributions to minorities that justify negative behavior toward them.

The justification for discriminating against a member of a stereotyped group need not come from the behavior of the target. It can also come from the situation, as Gaertner and Dovidio (1977) demonstrated. These researchers based their study on the well-documented finding that people are less likely to offer help (presumably because they feel less responsible) when they believe there are other witnesses present. Gaertner and Dovidio reasoned that people should be especially prone to the "it's-not-my-responsibility" justification for not helping when the person in need is a member of another race. In their experiment, white participants believed they were listening to another participant, who was either white or black, over an intercom (they actually listened to prerecorded audiotapes). They also believed either that they were the only listeners or that there were two additional listeners on the intercom. After a while, the speaker appeared to be experiencing an emergency—participants heard her scream that a stack of chairs was falling on her. Participants who believed that they were the only witnesses to this emergency were slightly more likely to help the victim if she was black than if she was white. In marked contrast, participants who believed that they were one of three witnesses to this emergency, and hence had a nonracial excuse for not helping, were much less likely to help the victim if she was black than if she was white. It would appear that participants' failure to show comparable discrimination when they lacked a good excuse stemmed from their motivation to avoid being or appearing prejudiced.

Sometimes psychological cover for discrimination is built into the structure of the situation (see Batson, Flink, Schoenrade, Fultz, & Pych, 1986; Snyder et al., 1979). One such experimental paradigm (a variant of one described in Chapter 1) works as follows: White participants arrive at the laboratory and are informed that they will be evaluating a movie playing on one of two monitors separated by a partition. The experimenter then asks the participant to take a seat in front of one of the two monitors. Already sitting in front of each of the monitors is a confederate who is either black or white. The critical manipulation is whether both monitors show the same movie or two different ones. Although many whites presumably wish to avoid sitting with the black, only those in the two-movie condition were comfortable acting upon this feeling. The reason for this is that the two-movie condition, unlike the one-movie condition, renders the motivation for the participant's seating choice ambiguous: it could either reflect the illicit motive of wishing to avoid the black or the more legitimate motive of genuinely preferring the movie being shown on the monitor watched by the white.

Race-Neutral Beliefs   Earlier we noted that whites' negative affect toward blacks often manifests itself in their support of social policies that prevent blacks from achieving full membership in mainstream American society. Whites are comfortable taking these positions, according to many theories of prejudice, because they can rationalize their positions as not really about blacks but about principle. In opposing school busing as a means of achieving racial integration, for example, a white might claim without compunction that "It's not the blacks, it's the buses" (Fiske, 1998). Even when they admit to negative beliefs about blacks, however, whites still may not feel that they are prejudiced if they rationalize these beliefs as reflecting not blacks' essential inferiority but their violation of traditional values of self-reliance, responsibility, hard work, and so on. Thinking negatively of others because of their skin color is unacceptable, but thinking negatively of others because of their personal or group faults apparently is not. From the perspective of many whites, then, expressing a belief such as "It's really a matter of some people not trying hard enough; if blacks would only try harder, they could be just as well off as whites" (Pettigrew & Meertens, 1995) does not make them prejudiced. After all, the argument goes, this belief does not assume that blacks are essentially inferior, only that they do not act in accordance with American values.

The Liberating Effects of Moral Credentials

Consider the situation of a white who must choose between a white and a black for a position or an award. Whites in this circumstance frequently experience discomfort, knowing that they will be vulnerable to charges of racism should they select the white candidate. Their dilemma is especially acute if they believe that the white candidate's credentials are superior: Should they act on their true preference, thereby risking the charge of racism, or should they provide the politically correct answer, thereby misrepresenting their true attitudes and possibly making a suboptimal choice? One factor that can liberate people to act upon their true attitudes in such situations is independent evidence that they are not racist. To the extent that they can point to such evidence that they are not racist, they will be less worried that expressing their preference for the white candidate would be interpreted as racist. "Moral credentials" of this type are most available to individuals who customarily behave in a nonprejudiced fashion. However, even prejudiced individuals sometimes engage in ostensibly nonprejudiced behavior, if only out of deference to the anti-prejudice norms—and thus they too can establish (and be liberated by) moral credentials.

An experiment by Fein et al. (2002) supports this reasoning. In this study, white participants' confidence in their egalitarian credentials was boosted by informing them that a questionnaire they had taken earlier revealed that they were low in racism. Participants then evaluated two résumés, one of a strong white job applicant, and one of a somewhat weaker black applicant. Participants who had just been informed that they were low in racism, and who were therefore secure in their belief that their judgments were unlikely to be taken as prejudiced, were less likely to express a preference for the black candidate over the stronger white candidate. These participants, confident in their egalitarian credentials, relaxed their efforts to avoid prejudice and were willing to express negativity that they otherwise would have curtailed (Kunda & Spencer, 2003).

To establish moral credentials, it is not necessary to receive accreditation from others, as in Fein et al.'s study. One's track record alone often is sufficient, as research by Monin and Miller (2001) reveals. One of their studies required participants to make two job recruitment-related decisions. The first of these asked participants to indicate which of five applicants they would choose for a "starting position" in a "large consulting firm." The candidates were briefly described by means of a picture, name, college, GPA, and major. In all conditions, the fourth applicant was designed to be the most attractive: He or she had graduated from a prestigious institution, had majored in economics, and had the highest GPA.

The manipulated variable was the race of that star applicant. In one condition he was an African-American male, whereas in the other condition he was a white male. The target's race was manipulated by changing his photograph. The four other applicants were always white males. Following the completion of the first recruitment task–in which virtually all participants chose the star applicant–and a series of unrelated questions, participants were faced with a second task that asked them how strongly they would recommend a black for a job in a hostile (i.e., racist) work environment. The job description was written so that even nonprejudiced participants would be reluctant to recommend a black for this job, simply out of concern for his well-being. This reluctance was not expected to overcome their fear of appearing prejudiced, however, unless they had established their credentials as a nonprejudiced person. The results revealed this to be the case: Only those participants given the opportunity to select a black candidate in the first recruitment task were willing to say that they would not recommend a black for the second position.

Not everyone who is liberated by moral credentials is prejudiced. In the situation created by Monin and Miller, participants were reluctant to recommend a black not because they did not want him to secure a good job but because they did not want to see him in an uncomfortable situation. The reason that participants who lacked moral credentials overrode their misgivings and recommended him for the job anyway was because they feared being seen as prejudiced.

Monin and Miller's research also addresses a question left open in previous research. Namely, do moral credentials, and possibly situational ambiguity, liberate people because they leave them feeling more confident that they are not prejudiced or merely more confident that they will not appear prejudiced? In order to determine if the credentialing effect was at least partially the result of participants' feeling more confident that they were unprejudiced, Monin and Miller conducted one version of their procedure in which the participant believed that the experimenter who collected the responses to the second job recommendation was unaware of their previous actions (i.e., credentials). If credentials work solely by reducing people's fear that they will appear prejudiced, it should be critical that the second audience knows of their previous behavior. On the other hand, if credentials' power derives at least partially from reassuring people that they (and hence their actions) are not motivated by prejudice, then it should not matter if the second audience is unaware of their credentials. This is just what Monin and Miller found, suggesting that people censor themselves at least some of the time because of their concern with actually being prejudiced—not just appearing prejudiced.

Reverse Discrimination   Monin and Miller's research also highlights another aspect of behavioral ambiguity. As we saw earlier, the presence of a potential nonrace-related motive (e.g., preference for a particular movie) can liberate people to act upon their negative affect toward members of another race. Monin and Miller's research shows that the presence of a potential race-related motive can constrain people from acting upon other motives (e.g., concern for the well-being of a member of another race). The latter dynamic can even result in preferential treatment for minority members in some situations. Instances of so-called reverse discrimination occur when actors fear that treating a minority member as they would a majority member could be attributed to prejudice. Dutton's (1971) investigation of dress code enforcement at upscale restaurants illustrates this phenomenon. When couples arrived at the restaurants with the male wearing attire that was slightly too casual (a turtleneck sweater), they were nearly twice as likely to be seated when they were black as when they were white. Although the hosts had a perfectly valid reason to refuse admission to the black couples (the absence of a tie), they were not secure enough to risk having their refusal attributed to prejudice.

Summing Up

Most people go to considerable lengths to avoid acting or thinking in a prejudiced manner. One reason for this is that most forms of prejudice—especially racial prejudice—are socially sanctioned or even legally proscribed. A second reason is that most people's good opinion of themselves requires that they not be prejudiced. People's quest to avoid acting, speaking, or thinking in a prejudiced manner inevitably involves self-censorship. People must constantly be ready to censor the impulse to direct words or acts toward a social group or its members that could be interpreted as prejudiced.

One theme of this chapter concerns people's ability to censor prejudiced thoughts and feelings. Negativity is more easily expunged from some aspects of behavior than from others. People are less able to inhibit their negative feelings toward a social group in their nonverbal than in their verbal behavior. Controlling our thoughts is more difficult still, but recent evidence suggests that even stereotypic thoughts—once assumed to be automatically activated by any relevant social cue—can be suppressed and prevented from entering into consciousness. Additional evidence suggests that people also can prevent themselves from applying already-activated stereotypes.

A second theme of this chapter focuses on the conditions under which people express rather than censor their prejudiced feelings. Whites are much more inclined to express their anti-black feelings when they can do so without fear of being labeled prejudiced. For example, when negative behavior toward an individual black could be interpreted as reflecting factors other than racial attitudes—and hence could not definitively be labeled as racially motivated—it is much less likely to be censored. The psychology of self-censorship in the domain of prejudice thus has two components: People inhibit the expression of prejudice, but they also attempt to express it, sometimes unconsciously, in ways that leave them secure in their nonprejudiced self-image.

Chapter Review

1. What are three ways to explain the drop in anti-black attitudes expressed in the United States from the 1960s to today? What explanation seems most plausible? Present evidence for your choice.
2. Explain why one cannot understand prejudice without understanding the role that self-censorship plays in its experience and expression.
3. Describe each of the following ways of measuring prejudice: subtle explicit measures, nonverbal measures, and implicit measures. What are the advantages and disadvantages of using each type of measure?
4. Explain the basic ideas of spreading activation theory (SAT). Using SAT, what is the pattern of data needed to conclude that one has an implicit prejudice? Describe in concrete terms how Fazio et al.'s research provides evidence that whites associate blacks with negativity.
5. This chapter suggests that we can control (at least somewhat) what we say, do, think, and feel. Provide evidence that individuals may be able to control each of these four modes of expression. In addition, compare and contrast how difficult it is to control each of these expressions of prejudice.
6. Describe three types of conditions under which people would feel free to express negative prejudice yet would not feel that they had acted in a prejudiced manner.
7. How do "moral credentials" serve to liberate people to express negativity? Are people liberated because they believe that they will not appear prejudiced or because they themselves are reassured that they are not prejudiced? Present evidence that supports your conclusion.
8. Describe how the audience (black or white) affects individuals' various expressions of anti-black prejudice.

Going Beyond the Chapter

1. This chapter states that "in light of whites' discriminatory behavior towards blacks in anonymous situations, it seems unlikely that their nondiscriminatory treatment of them in face-to-face situations is entirely genuine." Could

it be that both behaviors are equally genuine? What are other possible ways to explain the differing behavior across these two situations?

2. Given what you know about the expression and censorship of anti-black prejudice, do you think that the same processes would hold for prejudice based on gender, weight, sexual orientation, age, or disability? Do you agree that "it appears that prejudice is prejudice." Compare and contrast how you think that prejudice is censored and expressed for these various groups.

3. How consciously or unconsciously do individuals self-censor their expressions of prejudice? Do people play an active role in censoring the prejudice they express? Or do individuals' actions instead reflect passive inaction? How can the studies that you read about help you to disentangle these possible interpretations?

4. Social etiquette likely varies across cultures. Consider how the censorship and expression of prejudice would vary cross-culturally. Would the processes differ? If so, in what ways? Would there be cultural differences in the particular prejudices that would need to be censored? Even within a culture, there might be differences in terms of what is acceptable: general societal norms in the United States, for example, but also more local, regional, or subcultural norms. How would the censorship and expression of prejudice vary across different subcultures in the United States? Would the same processes hold?

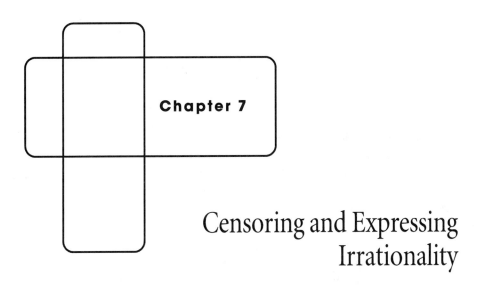

Chapter 7

Censoring and Expressing
Irrationality

We all know chocolate lovers. You may be one yourself. If you are, imagine that someone offered you a choice of two chocolates alike in all respects except for shape. One is shaped like a heart and the other like a cockroach. Which one would you choose? If you are like most people, you would probably be put off, possibly even repulsed, by the sight of the chocolate cockroach and would opt for the chocolate heart. Now imagine that you were offered your choice of two chocolates that differed in two respects. As before, one is shaped like a cockroach and the other a heart, but now the two chocolates also differ in size and value: the chocolate heart is small (worth 50 cents) whereas the chocolate cockroach is large (worth $2). Which of these would you choose? When Christopher Hsee (1999) presented college students with this choice, he found that the majority (64%) actually chose the chocolate cockroach.

Why would the majority of people opt for a chocolate that so obviously repulsed them? Did the larger size of the chocolate cockroach really compensate for its repulsiveness? Possibly, but the theme of this chapter suggests another explanation. Namely, people are disposed to censor their private impulses and feelings (disgust, in this case) when they feel that acting upon them would be irrational.

Maximizing Monetary Value Over
Psychological Well-being

In the last chapter we saw how the fear of either being or being seen as prejudiced leads people to censor their thoughts and actions. This chapter considers the impact that the fear of either being or being seen as irrational has on the self-censorship process. As in the case of prejudice, the process we consider here is one in which people conform not so much to other people as to cultural ideals of appropriate conduct. Our culture teaches us that we should not be prejudiced and that we should not be irrational. We all have irrational feelings from time to time, but we are expected to keep them in check and prevent them from dominating more rational considerations. It is acceptable to acknowledge that you are disgusted by the thought of eating a chocolate shaped like a cockroach, but it is not acceptable to allow this irrational feeling to prevent you from selecting a clearly superior chocolate.

Censoring Feelings of Disgust

Let us return to the case of chocolate preferences. Chocolate lovers can point to many features that they believe differentiate the relative tastiness of chocolates (filling, color, texture, etc.), thereby justifying their preferences for some chocolates over others. One feature of chocolates that even chocoholics are unlikely to emphasize, however, is shape. This is not to say that shape doesn't influence chocolate preference, only that it isn't a factor that people believe should dominate other, more legitimate dimensions of preference, such as size.

It should also be said that people will not always choose the larger of two chocolates. For example, if the larger of two proffered chocolates had recently been handled by the grimy fingers of a chocolate-loving young child, people would likely have no trouble opting for the smaller, hygienically safer alternative. In this case, the person's feelings of disgust, having an objective basis, would be seen as a legitimate basis for choosing the smaller chocolate. The case of the chocolate cockroach is quite different. The feelings of disgust that it elicited did not have an objective basis and, thus, however strong these feelings might be, they could not justify taking the smaller chocolate. As a result, the majority of people in Hsee's experiment censored their feelings of disgust and opted for a chocolate that they did not want (and very likely wouldn't even eat) rather than admit to someone, perhaps even to themselves, that they were influenced by something that could not rationally be linked to either safety or gastronomic pleasure.

Faced with a conflict between a preferred course of action and a less preferred but objectively superior one, people often choose the latter. Censoring their true preferences in these situations may enable people to avoid feeling or looking irrational, but it often leaves them less happy.

Censoring Feelings of Resentment

The sense of unfairness is another example of emotion that people feel should not dictate their decisions even though it plays a large role in determining their satisfaction with decision outcomes. Feelings of unfairness arise in many circumstances but especially ones in which we receive less of some resource (e.g., pay, affection, chocolates) than others around us do. So unpleasant are feelings of injustice that people try hard to avoid situations that put them at risk for such feelings.

A simple demonstration of this point is provided by Blount and Bazerman (1996). These researchers approached participants in a psychology experiment with the invitation of participating in a second experiment conducted by a colleague. One group of potential participants was offered $7 to participate in the 40-minute experiment, knowing that all participants would be receiving $7. A second group was offered $8 to participate in the 40-minute experiment, knowing that some participants were arbitrarily (based on the last digit of their social security number) being offered $10. Even though they were being paid more ($8 vs. $7) for the same work, substantially more of the students presented with the "just" arrangement agreed to participate than did students presented with the "unjust" arrangement (72% vs. 55%). The difference in participation rates would seem to make a simple point about the students. They realized that their psychological well-being would be affected not only by the size of their compensation but also by its fairness. The $8 offer was larger than the $7 offer, but it was also less fair—and as a consequence was less attractive.

Few people have difficulty admitting that unfairness bothers them. For example, faced with a choice between two equally well-paid jobs that do not differ in any respect save the fairness of the wage (e.g., in one job the pay was the same as that of coworkers and in the other it was 10% less), few people would hesitate to choose the fair work situation. But how comfortable would people be choosing a fair work situation over an unfair one if the latter actually paid more? A second condition in Blount and Bazerman's study addressed this question. Here, rather than being presented with only one of the two options just described, participants were presented with both options and had to choose between them. Did students still express less attraction to the unfair wage in this condition? No, they did not. Given a choice between the two experiments, only 16% opted to participate in the experiment in which everyone received $7, as compared to 56% who opted to participate in the experiment in which they received $8 and others received $10 (28% chose not to participate in either).

Why did fairness seem so much more important to people when they only saw one of the options than when they saw both? Actually, the fairness of the wage likely remained as important to students faced with the choice between the options; what changed was that here they feared they would look soft headed and irrational if they based their choice on concerns of fairness. Participants seemed to feel they should "suck it up" and do the smart thing—accept the higher-paying experiment even though they anticipated (probably correctly) that it would leave them feeling resentful. They would rather put themselves in a situation in which they knew they would be unhappy than be accused of losing sight of the all-important bottom line.

A study by Tversky and Griffin (1991) provides another example of decision makers' censoring their feelings of injustice. In this study college students were asked to imagine that they planned to work for one year before returning to college and had received two offers that were identical in compensation and workload. The only difference was in office size. Specifically, the participants read:

> Company A gives you a small (100 square-foot) office, and gives another employee (who has similar qualifications to you) an equally small office. Company B gives you a medium size (170 square-feet) office but gives another employee (who has similar qualifications to you) a large (240 square-feet) office.

Tversky and Griffin asked one group of students to predict which position would leave them happier and a second group to indicate which position they would choose. The majority (66%) of the first group predicted greater happiness in Company A (with small office for self and others), but the majority (57%) of the second group chose to work at Company B (with medium office for self and larger office for others). Relative office size may affect workers' psychological well-being and they may even be comfortable choosing a job on the basis of this factor, all other things being equal. However, weighing relative office size more than absolute office size in a job decision would make people look irrational, which they were not prepared to do.

Censoring Feelings of Unfairness

A sense of injustice arises not only when people receive less of some resource than they think they deserve, but also when they think that others have treated them with less respect or dignity than they deserve (Miller, 2001). For example, our sense of fairness requires that those in authority provide us with rationales for their decisions and listen to our thoughts and concerns

(Tyler & Lind, 1992). So important is the respectfulness of the treatment we receive from authorities that its absence can leave us unhappy even if we benefit from the exchange.

People may be comfortable acknowledging that they prefer respectful to disrespectful treatment if getting such treatment does not cost them anything. But what if a gain in respectful treatment only came at a cost in material benefits? Would respect-valuing people still be comfortable pursuing respectful treatment? A study by Bazerman and his colleagues (Bazerman, Schroth, Shah, Diekmann, & Tensbrunsel, 1994) pitted procedural justice against salary maximization to answer this question. These researchers presented soon-to-be graduating MBA students with a hypothetical employment decision that mirrored one they would soon be facing in real life. Participants were assigned to one of two conditions. Participants in one condition read descriptions of six hypothetical job offers, one at a time, and in each case designated whether they would accept the job offer or reject the offer and remain on the market (accepting one offer did not preclude accepting any other offers since they were independent decisions). Participants in another condition read descriptions of three pairs of job offers, one pair at time, and for each pair designated whether they would accept one of the job offers or reject both and thus remain on the market. Following are slightly abbreviated versions of two of the job offers:

> The **first** offer is from Company A for $75, 000 a year. Company A is a leading consulting firm. MBA graduates enter the firms as associates and begin working directly with clients. New associates are assigned by senior partners to specific clients, projects, and engagement teams in which a senior partner is in charge. Decisions involving company policies such as training and job objectives are made by senior management. In general, new associates are not encouraged to voice their opinions or objections.
>
> The **second** offer is from Company B for $60,000 a year. As a prominent consulting firm, Company B helps corporations manage the problems and opportunities created by change. New associates are given the opportunity to participate in decisions such as training and job objectives. Upon arrival, new associates are allowed to voice their preferences regarding client and project assignments. The firms encourages all consultants, both junior and senior, to voice their opinions for changes and improvements to the company's policies.

When the jobs described here were presented one at a time, the majority (73%) of MBA students who accepted one of the two jobs accepted Company B. In contrast, when the jobs were presented as a pair, the majority (62%)

of the MBA students who accepted one of the two jobs accepted Company A. The first result suggests that even these hard-headed MBAs cared about relational issues and valued more the respectful treatment afforded by Company B than the greater compensation offered by Company A. The second result, however, suggested that these same MBAs apparently were not comfortable with the idea that they cared more about respect and autonomy than cold cash, and so they chose to override their personal preferences and opt for a job that they ultimately expected would leave them less satisfied (Hsee, Zhang, Yu, and Xi, 2003).

Consider one more example of people's tendency to choose one action over another even when they know it will bring them less satisfaction—simply because it is the rational thing to do. The study identified a large national sample of Americans who indicated that they had at some time considered suing over an injury that caused them to miss at least a day of their normal activity (Tyler, Huo, & Lind, 1999). The participants were asked what compensation they expected to get from their claim and how fairly they expected they would be treated during the litigation process. They were also asked whether they ultimately decided to initiate litigation, and if so, what the outcome was and how well they were treated during the process. Finally, they were asked how satisfied they were with their decision to sue.

The results indicated that people's decision about whether or not to pursue an injury claim was influenced strongly by their expectations of financial gain. The more likely they thought they were to win and the more money they thought they would win, the more likely they were to sue. Expectation of fair treatment during the litigation process did not affect whether or not they decided to initiate the process. Even when people expected to be treated unfairly by the process, they were disposed to sue if they thought the prospects for financial gain were good. On the other hand, people's feelings of satisfaction with their decision at the completion of the process were highly dependent on how fairly they thought they had been treated. In fact, perceived fairness of treatment was more strongly related to postoutcome satisfaction than was degree of financial gain. Regardless of whether or not they won or how much they won, people were happier with the process if they felt it treated them fairly.

Here, as in the previously described research, we see people making decisions that minimize rather than maximize their satisfaction. People may know how important relational considerations (e.g., fair treatment) are in determining how satisfied they will be with their decisions, but they are uncomfortable letting that knowledge inform their decisions. It is soft headed to be concerned about fairness or other "soft" factors at the expense of "hard" factors such as material gain. Caring about fairness is one thing, but letting concerns about fairness override your better judgment is quite another.

Censoring Feelings of Embarrassment

To the extent that people feel deviant when acting on preferences that diverge from so-called rational standards, we should expect them to be especially "rational" when their decisions are open to public scrutiny. An experiment by Brown (1970) supports this conjecture. College student participants were recruited for what they thought was a perception experiment in which they were to "sense" an object for 3 minutes and develop detailed impressions of it—shape, texture, surface smoothness, and so on. The object participants were instructed to sense (suck, lick, and bite) was a 4-inch rubber pacifier. Once they had spent 3 minutes sensing the pacifier in privacy, the experimenter told participants it was now time to describe the experience to an audience. Their description could take any of four forms: (1) a live presentation, (2) a videotape recording, (3) an audiotape recording, or (4) a written statement. Supposedly to encourage variety in the chosen mode of description, the experimenter had randomly decided on different amounts of compensation for the different options. These payoff rates (bear in mind this was 1970) were $1.50 for the live presentation, $1.00 for the videotape recording, $.50 for the audiotape, and $.00 for the written statement. The audience (two male confederates) to which they were to give their presentation in whatever mode they chose was seated at the other end of the laboratory. There was one more experimental manipulation: Half of the participants were told that the audience knew of the payoff rate and half were told the audience was not informed of the payoff rate.

As the experimenters hoped, the college students found it uncomfortable to spend 3 minutes with a pacifier in their mouth and they were even more uncomfortable to have to talk about it to strangers. Moreover, the embarrassment they felt in describing the experience increased as the degree of public exposure increased. Even though making a live presentation to the audience was more lucrative than simply providing the audience with a written description, more participants elected to do the latter than the former. This result is hardly surprising: In the participants' eyes, the compensation differential did not offset the embarrassment differential. Although the offer of greater compensation was not sufficient to get participants to make a public or videotape presentation, the knowledge that the audience knew of the compensation rates was. Almost twice as many people chose to make a public presentation when the audience supposedly knew that it paid more than when the audience supposedly had no such knowledge. Participants apparently felt that letting embarrassment get in the way of making money would make them look even more foolish to an audience than would talking to them about the experience of sucking a pacifier.

Reflection Increases Rationality But Not Satisfaction

Simply asking people to think about (rather than justify or publicize) the reasons for their choices appears sufficient to shift their attention toward "rational" considerations and away from factors that are more predictive of ultimate satisfaction. Wilson and Schooler (1991) provided an especially interesting demonstration of this effect. Their study involved introductory psychology students at the University of Virginia who volunteered for a study entitled "Choosing College Courses." The sign-up sheet indicated that participants would receive detailed information about all of the 200-level courses being offered by the psychology department the following semester. Participants were run in large groups during the period when students registered for the classes they wanted to take the following semester.

Students were told that the study's purpose was to "look at some issues in decision making of interest to psychologists, such as how people make decisions between alternatives." They received descriptions of the nine 200-level psychology courses. Each description provided detailed information about the course, including the name of the professor, the requirements for the psychology major satisfied by the course, the format of the course (lecture or discussion), previous course evaluations, and a description of the course content. Some students (the control condition) were simply instructed to read the information about the nine courses carefully and then rate the likelihood that they would take each course. Another group of students (the rating condition) were asked "to stop and think about each piece of information about every course and then to indicate the extent to which it made them more or less likely to take the course."

The results were complex but telling. Most interesting was the discrepancy between the importance participants assigned to course evaluations in making their decisions and the impact course ratings had on the control group's course selections. The results from the control participants indicated that course ratings strongly influenced their course selections, which made sense because these ratings were strong predictors of students' ultimate satisfaction with the course. This was not true of students required to rate the factors first. For them, other seemingly more substantial or legitimate factors (e.g., course format, course content) loomed larger in deciding which courses to take. Generalizing from this study, it appears that reflecting upon the reasons for their decisions leads people to focus primarily on those attributes that seem *plausible* and *legitimate* reasons for liking (disliking) the object of concern rather than on those attributes that *actually* influence liking (disliking) for it.

The Legitimating Impact of Self-interest

Our focus to this point has been people's tendency to censor their impulses when they fear acting upon them will make them appear irrational. One consequence is that people look more rational (less soft-headed) than they are. But looking rational does not always require people to refrain from acting upon irrational impulses (i.e., ones that do not seem to reflect bottom-line-style reasoning). People often indulge their irrational impulses while still appearing to be acting rationally. One way they do this is through the reasons they give for their decisions or actions.

Emphasizing Self-interest in Accounts for Behavior

Many times the rationality of a choice is defined by the person's reasons for making it rather than by the choice itself. For this reason, we often find people providing rational reasons for choices they made on "irrational" grounds. This is especially likely to be the case where the rationality of the behavior is more ambiguous than it was in the cases we have described thus far.

Consider the decision facing a voter about whether she should vote for or against an incumbent politician—say, the president. To know what the rational decision is for this voter, we need to know more about her, most notably whether her circumstances have improved or deteriorated during the incumbent's term. It would be rational for the person to vote for the incumbent if her material circumstances had improved during his term but not if they had deteriorated. Actually, the evidence suggests that personal economic circumstances have a surprisingly small impact on people's voting behavior (Kinder, 1998). It is popular to claim that people "vote their pocketbook," but pocketbook voters are difficult to find.

As an illustration, consider findings from a study known as the National Election Study that surveys a large sample of Americans about their voting behavior every four years (Sears & Funk, 1990). One of the questions that the survey asks of voters is whether they are "better off" or "worse off" than they were four years ago. How people answer this question usually reveals little connection to their reported choice of presidential candidate. Many people who say they are worse off indicate that they will vote (have voted) for the incumbent, and many who are better off indicate that they will not vote (have not voted) for the incumbent. The only circumstance in which a strong relation is found between these two measures is when the measures are collected in exit polls (rather than weeks or months before or after the election) (Sears & Lau, 1983; Stein, 1990).

People seem uncomfortable telling an interviewer both that they just voted for the incumbent and that their circumstances have declined during his presidency; similarly, they seem uncomfortable telling an interviewer both that they just voted against the incumbent and that their circumstances have improved during his presidency. Whether the misreporting that occurs in exit polls involves people misrepresenting their economic circumstances so as to bring them into line with their vote or vice versa is unclear. Whatever the case, people leaving a polling booth appear reluctant to acknowledge to an interviewer that they voted contrary to their economic self-interests.

As an aside, it should be noted that the weak relationship observed between self-interest and voting behavior does not mean that casting a vote is an unpredictable, arbitrary act. Voters may not weigh their own problems heavily when deciding for whom to vote, but research shows that voters do weigh heavily their sense of whether the circumstances of the country as a whole are improving or not (Kinder & Kiewet, 1981). Rather than asking of incumbents, "What have you done for me lately?" they more often appear to ask, "What have you done for the nation lately?"

People also seem disposed to exaggerate the relation between their attitudes toward public policies and their stake in the policy. An interesting example is provided by a study conducted in the early 1970s in which researchers examined attitudes toward a controversial social program that involved "busing" children from one area to another as a means of assuring a racial balance in public schools. Various surveys at the time sought to determine the basis of people's attitudes toward this issue. The most relevant group for the present discussion is whites who opposed the policy.

Consistent with other findings, there was little evidence that self-interest played a big role in whites' opposition to school busing. For example, white opponents of the policy were no more likely to be parents of children who would be affected than were white supporters. Anti-black attitudes and especially hostility toward government intervention in community life were much more predictive of opposition than any indicator of material risk (Green & Cowden, 1992; Sears & Funk, 1990). The finding most pertinent to the present discussion, however, was the accounts given by white opponents of busing when asked to explain their opposition. Their accounts focused on narrowly defined self-interest arguments: concern for their children's safety, diminished property values, inconvenience to kids, and so forth (Sears & Funk, 1990). Whites may have been comfortable acknowledging to an interviewer that they were opposed to busing, but they were not comfortable offering an account for that opposition that did not focus on their material self-interest. Even when their opposition was not grounded in self-interest, they made it sound as though it were.

A similar point can be made about attitudes toward many other social policies. People's attitudes often are based much more on principle, and less on economic calculus or "hard" facts, than their accounts suggest to be the case. Consider attitudes toward capital punishment. Supporters of capital punishment emphasize its deterrent effect; whereas opponents emphasize its ineffectiveness and costliness, along with its discriminatory application. However, presenting evidence that undermines these rational reasons is notoriously unsuccessful in changing people's minds, suggesting that more elemental feelings of justice and retribution underlie people's attitudes (Gross & Ellsworth, 2003; Vidmar & Ellsworth, 1974).

Concealing Compassion Within the Guise of Self-interest

People's motivation to make their actions appear rational and consistent with their interests may even extend to their pro-social acts. It may seem strange that people would want to have those actions of theirs that benefit another viewed as guided by self-interest rather than a nobler motive, but there is growing evidence that this is the case. For example, on the basis of extensive interviews and surveys, Wuthnow (1991) claimed that although Americans actually engage in many acts of genuine compassion in their daily lives, they are loath to acknowledge that these acts were motivated by genuine compassion or kindness. Instead, people offer pragmatic or instrumental reasons for them, saying things such as, "It gave me something to do," or "It got me out of the house." Indeed, Wuthnow claimed that the people he interviewed went out of their way to stress that they were not a "bleeding heart," "goody two-shoes," or "do-gooder."

Earlier we saw that people feel uncomfortable voting for a candidate merely because they think it is the right thing to do. Wuthnow's results suggest that they also feel uncomfortable helping others merely because it is the right thing to do. In fact, one's image as a good and just person may not be compromised as much by pursuing self-interest as one's image as a reasonable person is compromised by unconditionally pursuing justice. The cynicism reflected in the expression "Scratch an altruist and you'll find an egoist" undoubtedly has some validity, as people will often claim to be acting altruistically when they are not. On the other hand, there seems to be growing evidence for the validity of another expression: "Scratch an egoist and you'll find an altruist."

Interestingly, the claim that people—at least Americans—often conceal their more noble sentiments under the guise of self-interest is not new. Over 150 years ago, the French social philosopher Alexis de Tocqueville observed that "Americans . . . enjoy explaining almost every act of their lives on the principle of self-interest. . . . I think that in this they often do themselves less than justice, for sometimes in the United States, as elsewhere, one sees people carried away by the . . . spontaneous impulses natural to man. But the Americans are hardly prepared to admit that they do give way to emotions of this sort" (1969/1835/, p. 546).

What are we to make of people's tendency to emphasize the benefits they receive by helping others? One possibility is that because our culture values individualism over collectivism, people worry, perhaps appropriately, that appearing too sociocentric will make them suspect in the eyes of others (Ratner & Miller, 2001). To the extent this is true, accounts for pro-social actions that emphasize self-interest, rather than diminishing the actions, actually may normalize or license them.

Pointing to Self-interest to Justify Morally Questionable Behavior

Sometimes the mere availability of a self-interested account can neutralize a potentially discrediting action, as is demonstrated by one of the most famous experiments in social psychology (Festinger & Carlsmith, 1959). This study tested the hypothesis that when people engage in actions that are discrepant from their attitudes—and they perceive no justification for the discrepancy—they will experience an aversive state called cognitive dissonance. People experiencing this state are presumed to be motivated to reduce it, which they can do by bringing their attitudes into line with their behavior. The experiment created an attitude-behavior discrepancy for participants by inducing them to tell the "next subject" that the exceedingly boring experiment they had just participated in was, in fact, very interesting. It was predicted that participants who could not justify expressing a belief that deviated so dramatically from the one they privately held would be motivated to change their private belief in the direction of their public expression so as to reduce cognitive dissonance. No such belief change was predicted when participants could justify the discrepancy between what they said and what they privately believed.

At this point, please turn your attention not to the account of dissonance arousal or dissonance reduction, but to the recipe the researchers used to create the special conditions necessary to test their hypothesis. Creating these conditions required an experimental dynamic that was sufficiently powerful to induce participants to act counter to their true attitudes (lie about the interestingness of the experiment) yet was not perceived to be sufficiently powerful to do so. Remember, if people acknowledge the power of the situational forces operating on them, there would be no dissonance.

The dynamic that these researchers used is one that exploits social etiquette, the power and workings of which we described in Chapter 2. Although the experimenter offered the participants monetary compensation for their lie ($1 in the "insufficient justification" condition vs. $20 in the "sufficient justification" condition), what really induced subjects to comply was their wish to avoid challenging the experimenter's definition of the situation, in particular his apparent view that what he was asking the subject to do (help him by leading the next subject to think the experiment was interesting) was an appropriate request. Rather than causing a scene by challenging the face of the experimenter, participants agreed to tell a lie.

But compliance with the dictates of social etiquette apparently was not perceived to provide sufficient justification for their action. We know this because participants who were paid a paltry $1 for the lie experienced dissonance, as revealed by their modification of their attitudes in a direction that made their action less discrepant—they reported greater genuine liking for the task that they had recommended to the other participant. On the other hand, participants appeared to view the offer of lavish compensation ($20—remember, these are 1958 dollars) to be sufficient justification for telling the lie. We know this because participants who were paid $20 still reported that they personally found the task boring after they had told their unsuspecting fellow participants that it was interesting. Thus material gain, while not motivating participants to tell the lie (concern with social etiquette did that), did console them for doing so.

Festinger and Carlsmith's experiment demonstrates that in our culture it is impermissible to comply in the so-called forced-compliance paradigm solely out of a desire to protect our face or that of the experimenter. If our culture did acknowledge social etiquette as a legitimate motivation for telling a lie, presumably Festinger and Carlsmith's procedure would not have generated dissonance even in the $1 condition. Interestingly, the fact that the effectiveness of the forced compliance paradigm relies so heavily on social etiquette as both a powerful force and one unrecognized or unaccepted as such may explain why this paradigm has proven ineffective for arousing cognitive dissonance among the Japanese (Miller & Prentice, 1994). One intriguing possible explanation for the ineffectiveness of this experimental paradigm in Japan is that Japanese culture's emphasis on interdependence over independence leads the Japanese (unlike Americans) to view social etiquette (like lavish compensation for Americans) as sufficient to induce one to act contrary to his or her true attitude.

Using Self-interest to Provide Psychological Cover

The claim that people are hesitant to act upon desires that do not comport with conventional conceptions of rationality suggests one way that people might be encouraged to act upon these impulses: namely, structure the situation so that the person can rationalize the action she wishes to undertake as being consistent with her self-interest. In fact, liberating people to act upon "irrational" impulses may not even require that they be given an unambiguous self-interested rationale for their action. Simply structuring the situation so that the motivation behind the action is ambiguous may suffice.

Appearing to Care about Money

Christopher Hsee (1995) provided one demonstration of how obscuring the self-interest-violating aspect of a person's true preference can increase the likelihood that the person will act upon that preference. Hsee recruited college students ostensibly to proofread text stored on computer files. The students were given a choice of two files to proofread: One contained boring furniture ads, the other more interesting personal ads. It seems likely that most students, all things being equal, would prefer to proofread the personal ads. The problem for the students, however, was that the pay (based on the number of errors detected) was actually higher for the furniture ads than the personal ads (there was supposedly an average of 9 errors per page on the furniture ads but only an average of 7 on the personal ads). Given this, it is not surprising that when asked how they would like to divide their minimum 10-page allotment, students overwhelmingly chose to work on the furniture ads over the personal ads (an average of 7.55 vs. 4.24 pages). Both the intrinsic and extrinsic value of an action may contribute to the appeal an activity has for a person, but if the two sources of satisfaction point in different directions, people feel compelled to censor the heart and follow the head in the direction of greater extrinsic value.

Hsee's experiment included another interesting condition. Here students were told that the error rate in the furniture ads varied from page to page (always at least 3 but could be as high as 15). It remained the case that the expected (though no longer certain) payment was greater if the students chose to work on the furniture ads, so if participants in the previously described condition chose the furniture ads because they genuinely cared about making more money (as opposed to simply wanting to appear to care), then participants in this condition should still prefer the furniture ads. On the other hand, if participants' preference for the furniture ads in the first condition only reflected their desire to appear appropriately sensitive to money, we are led to a different prediction. The fact that the pay is variable in this condition should give participants the necessary psychological cover for indulging their actual preference for the more appealing but less lucrative personal ads. True, the expected payment was greater for the furniture ads, but there was a chance they would actually get more money for proofreading the personal ads. They might reveal themselves to be gamblers by opting for the personal ads, but they would not reveal themselves to be voyeurs.

Indeed, students chose to proofread more pages of the personal ads than furniture ads (an average of 5.19 vs. 4.81) when the expected error rates (payments) were expressed in ranges than when they were expressed as fixed values. The likelihood remained that they would get more money by proofreading the boring material, but the fact that it was not inevitable was all the students needed to feel liberated to act upon their true preference.

The Exchange Fiction and Charitable Giving

We saw earlier instances of people attributing their pro-social acts to self-interest to avoid appearing motivated by compassion. In light of this effect, we might expect that people would welcome an opportunity that provided them with self-interested accounts for acting compassionately. In fact, this logic may, knowingly or unknowingly, underlie the practice of offering potential charity donors some product (e.g., light bulbs, return address labels, magazine subscriptions) in exchange for their donations. Certainly, the commonness of this practice suggests the net profit elicited by product-for-donation exchanges exceeds that elicited by strict charity appeals alone.

One explanation for the success of this strategy might be that the offer of an exchange creates a fiction that permits people to act on their impulse to help without committing themselves to unwanted psychological burdens, such as a public or private image as a "do-gooder" or an enduring, open-ended relationship with the victim group. In effect, the exchange fiction provides a psychological cover for individuals who wish to express their compassion and concerns with justice without having to reveal, or even recognize, their motives. When people receive a quid pro quo (e.g., a tax deduction or a token gift) for their assistance, they do not have to feel like a do-gooder. They can construe their action as something to feel good about but not as something that is inconsistent with collective representations of what constitutes acceptable forms of motivation.

In a test of the exchange fiction hypothesis, Holmes, Miller, and Lerner (2001) had a group of experimenters approach students on a university campus with one of a variety of charity appeals. The design was complicated, so only the most relevant conditions are discussed here. The key manipulations were the seriousness of the victims' need (high vs. low) and the presence or absence of an exchange (a decorative candle). In the *high-need* condition, donations were sought to help pay for a program designed to benefit emotionally disturbed children; in the *low-need* condition, they were sought to buy baseball equipment for a group of healthy 7- to 10-year-olds. The pattern of donation rates supported the prediction. When the victims' need was high (and so presumably was the sympathy they elicited), the offer of an exchange increased people's donation rate threefold; when the victims' need was low (and so presumably was the sympathy they elicited), the offer of an exchange had no significant effect.

The Holmes et al. (2001) study reveals the need for caution when interpreting the positive relationship between material incentives (e.g., tax deductions) and charitable donations. A straightforward interpretation of this finding is that people are disinclined to give if they are not compensated for doing so. This is certainly an accurate empirical description (people do give more when they are offered an incentive). However, it is not necessarily an accurate psychological interpretation. Incentives may serve not so much to motivate charitable giving as to legitimate it by providing a justification for it. The role of incentives as justifications rather than motivators comes into play when people already are motivated to help but are inhibited from doing so, as was the case for the individuals in the *high-need* condition of the Holmes et al. study.

The Growing Power of the Rationality Ideal

In the previous chapter we saw that norms against prejudice, especially racial prejudice, have grown stronger in America over the last 50 years. The same could be said about norms against irrationality or nonbottom-line thinking. Whether contemporary corporate leaders are more or less likely than their predecessors to exhort their corporate followers to act ethically is not easy to assess. What is clear, however, is that reasons corporate leaders give for acting ethically have changed. Ethical behavior, once encouraged as the right or moral thing to do, now is encouraged as the "smart" thing to do. "Ethics pay," as the familiar slogan puts it.

It is difficult to say precisely what social changes are responsible for people's growing fear of appearing irrational. What we can say is that one experience that leads people to act more in concert with their self-interest is taking a course in economics. The most extensive investigation of the impact of exposure to economic theory on decision making was conducted by Frank, Gilovich, and Regan (1993).

The specific question addressed by Frank et al. was this: Does exposing college students to the precepts and findings of economic theory (especially rational choice theory) influence the power they perceive self-interest to have, or at least should have, over their own lives and that of the average other? The researchers examined this question by assessing both at the beginning and end of the semester students' responses to two ethical dilemmas ("Would you return a lost envelope with $100 in it?" and "Would you report a billing error that benefited you?"). Students were members of either one of two different microeconomics classes or of a class unrelated to economics (astronomy). Of the economics classes, one was taught by an instructor who specialized in game theory (a field in which self-interest is axiomatic), the other by an instructor who specialized in economic development in Maoist China.

The results supported the hypothesis that studying economics fosters self-interest. Over the course of the semester, the responses of students in the game theorist's class became decidedly more self-interested (i.e., they were more likely to opt for not returning the lost money and not reporting the billing error). The responses of the students in the other economist's class also became more self-interested, though less so. There was virtually no change in the responses of the students in the control (astronomy) professor's class. Similar changes emerged on measures assessing students' expectations of the actions of the average person. In brief, exposing students to the theory that people's principal, even sole, motivation is self-interest left students more inclined to keep someone's lost $100 and less inclined to report a billing error (after all, to do otherwise would be to incur an "opportunity cost" in the jargon of economics).

The most significant finding of Frank et al. (1993) for the present analysis is that the experience of taking a course in microeconomics actually altered students' conceptions of the appropriateness of acting in a self-interested manner, not merely their definition of self-interest. Instruction in economics, it would appear, does not make cynics out of students by persuading them that the motivation behind people's actions, whatever it appears to be, is inevitably self-interest. Frank et al.'s (1993) participants did not emerge from Economics 101 believing that it actually is in one's self-interest to report a favorable billing error because, for example, it preempts guilt or fosters a reputation for honesty. Rather, they emerged apparently believing that not reporting a favorable billing error, in addition to being self-interested, is also the rational and appropriate action to take, however guilty one feels doing so.

Finally, educating people on the naturalness of acting on self-interest appears capable of undermining what many noneconomists would describe approvingly as "civic virtue." Brunk (1980) reported that exposing political science students to the rational choice model of voting behavior, which emphasizes the irrationality of voting (after all, the probability of being killed on the way to the polls is greater than the probability that your vote will matter), decreased the students' inclination to vote. People, it would appear, can be taught to act "naturally."

Summing Up

Individuals in Western cultures are increasingly disposed to censor their emotions or beliefs when expressing these convictions would make them seem irrational or insufficiently concerned with their economic self-interest. People's psychological well-being is frequently ill served by acting purely in terms of their economic self-interest, but they nevertheless often do just that. For example, even when people know that choosing one object over another will leave them feeling disgusted, resentful or otherwise dissatisfied, they may still choose it if that is what "bottom-line" reasoning dictates. And when people do act on their emotions, be they pro-or anti-social in origin, they tend to provide rational, self-interested accounts for their actions. People are much less comfortable giving moral or other emotion-based accounts for their actions than they are self-interested ones. In fact, just the anticipation of having to explain their actions makes people more likely to pursue options that are most easily explained by self-interest considerations. People appear more calculating and self-interested than they are in some cases because they have internalized the norm of self-interest, in others because they simply wish to avoid what they assume will be the disapproval of others if they violate it.

Chapter Review

1. Using the research by Blount and Bazerman, Tversky and Griffin, and Bazerman et al., provide evidence that people at times make decisions that will later make them resentful in order not to appear to be acting

irrationally. For each of the research examples, explain how participants' responses in each of the experimental conditions demonstrate this idea. Are there additional experimental conditions one could add to the different studies to gather more information to support this idea?

2. Explain how the role of public scrutiny illuminates people's motivations for censoring their behavior, using Brown's (1970) research as an example.

3. Examine Wilson and Schooler's study on thinking about the reasons for our choices.
   a. What were the experimental conditions they included to test their research ideas?
   b. Describe the methods they used.
   c. Describe their key findings.
   d. Explain why participants responded the ways they did in the various conditions.

4. Using the logic presented in the chapter, explain why individuals would want to conceal their true compassion or kindness and instead present their helping behavior as motivated by self-interest.

5. Using the notion of social etiquette, explain why participants in Festinger and Carlsmith's study agreed to lie in the various experimental conditions. Explain why this social etiquette account can help us understand cross-cultural differences in this experimental design. Why are American participants more likely than Japanese participants to change their attitudes to match their behavior when paid $1?

6. Describe the exchange fiction hypothesis. Explain how Holmes, Miller, and Lerner (2001) provide evidence for this hypothesis.

Going Beyond the Chapter

1. It seems curious that individuals do not want to be seen as altruistic but instead prefer others to see them as self-interested. Why do you think individuals want to be seen as self-interested? Is it to appear rational? Does coming off as soft or altruistic mean that one is seen as irrational? Do you think that individuals really think that they are self-interested, or do you think that they just want to appear to be self-interested? Justify your responses based on evidence in the chapter and your personal experiences.

2. This chapter focuses on the special conditions used in dissonance studies to create dissonance, emphasizing an account based on social etiquette. Can a social etiquette account fully explain why Festinger and Carlsmith found their pattern of results, or do you think that this account is incomplete? If so, in what ways?

3. In their research on the exchange fiction hypothesis, Holmes, Miller, and Lerner suggest that incentives may serve to justify charitable behavior rather than to motivate it. Are there conditions under which incentives motivate rather than justify helping? First, examine the conditions of their study to consider how they provide evidence that incentives justify rather than motivate pro-social behavior. Then propose future research that could help specify the different conditions under which incentives would function to motivate and to justify helping.

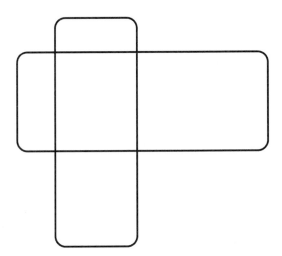

Epilogue

No book can claim to tell a reader everything there is to know about social psychology, and this one is no exception. Actually, given its briefness, this book's coverage has been especially selective. So what can a book that is so selective hope to convey to the reader about the field of social psychology? My goals were twofold.

First and foremost, I sought to provide the reader with an appreciation of the social psychologists' craft—to show how they think about the social world and how they translate their thoughts into empirical research. The book's restricted coverage has provided the opportunity to describe those studies that were covered, especially their historical context, method, and procedure, in more detail than is typical. I am especially happy to have been able to provide fuller than customary descriptions of a number of social psychology's classic studies. In my opinion, there is no better window into the art and science of this field than a detailed rendering of its classics.

My second objective has been to promote a more thematic view of social psychology than is customarily presented. It is true that capturing the richness, complexity, and diversity of social life in one or even a few overarching theories is not easy. Nevertheless, I believe that the social psychological take on social life has a coherence that both permits and benefits from thematic analysis. To this end, I have sought to show how much social psychology, especially classic social psychology, can be organized around, and illuminated by, the theme of self-censorship.

Along with providing an introduction to the field of social psychology, this book has offered an analysis of self-censorship—its motivations, forms, and consequences. I have tried especially to convey the pervasiveness and importance of self-censorship in daily life. It is frequently claimed that we are social products, and this is unquestionably true. The social world shapes our beliefs and feelings. But our experience of the social world also leads us to censor those beliefs and feelings from time to time. More than social products, we are social actors. Indeed, there would be no social world without social actors, and there would be no social actors without self-censorship.

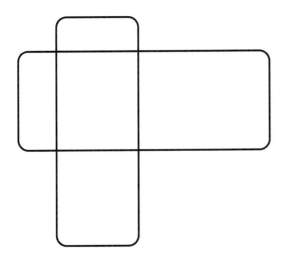

Appendix:
Research Summary Tables

Chapter 1: Introduction

RESEARCH SUMMARY TABLE 1			
Study	Citation	Key Concept	Key Finding
Vegetarians eating meat	Kitts (2003)	Individuals may censor themselves to preserve their group and their standing in it.	Students in vegetarian houses reported strong antimeat-eating norms, but the majority reported eating meat (usually fish) at times and also concealing their meat eating from their housemates.
Women's responses to conservative and liberal men	Zanna & Pack (1975)	Individuals may censor themselves to enhance their attractiveness to others.	Women expecting to meet an attractive conservative male presented themselves as more traditionally feminine and solved fewer anagram problems than those expecting to meet an attractive liberal male.
Men's responses to conservative and liberal women	Morier & Seroy (1994)	Individuals may censor themselves to enhance their attractiveness to others.	Replicating Zanna & Pack, males misrepresented the conservativeness of their sex-role attitudes to look appealing to an attractive woman.
Picking movies and gender	Bernstein, Stephenson, Snyder, & Wicklund (1983)	Individuals may censor themselves to avoid others' disapproval.	Men chose to sit next to an attractive woman more when different movies played on the two monitors than when the same movie was playing on both monitors.
A coin flip and an undesirable task	Batson, Thompson, Seuferling, Whitney, & Strongman (1999)	Individuals may censor themselves to remain true to their self-images.	In choosing between two tasks (one more desirable than the other), participants typically gave their partner the less desirable task. When the experimenter suggested flipping a coin to randomly assign the tasks, they tended to flip the coin, although they still generally gave themselves the desirable task. Only while looking in a mirror did they act fairly, following the actual results of the random coin toss.
Presenting positive and negative college experiences	Vorauer & Miller (1997)	Self-censorship may occur without awareness.	Participants described their college experiences to another person. If the other person presented a negative description, the participants presented a more negative description than if the other person had presented a positive description. Participants reported being unaware that they had altered their presentations.

Chapter 2: Social Etiquette

RESEARCH SUMMARY TABLE 2			
Study	Citation	Key Concept	Key Finding
Subway seats	Milgram & Sabini (1978)	We avoid challenging others' situational definitions.	Asked to give up their subway seats, the majority did. Only when the seat request was clearly illegitimate did they not generally comply.
Respecting others' situational definitions	Goffman (1959, 1971)	This work provides the conceptual foundation for the idea that challenging others' situational definitions is socially impolite.	Individuals want to respect or at least not challenge another's definition of a situation.
Give him a nickel!	Bushman (1988)	Individuals comply more often with requests from those in perceived roles of authority.	Individuals were more apt to give a stranger a nickel when asked by a women dressed in a uniform than a woman dressed as a panhandler or as a business executive.
Throwing Frisbees in Grand Central	Darley & Latané (1970)	Individuals are loath to challenge others' situational definitions of their situations.	Two individuals throwing a Frisbee brought in a third person who either did not respond, joined in enthusiastically, or angrily threw down the Frisbee. When the confederate either did not respond or was enthusiastic, others joined in. If the confederate responded angrily, others did not join in and often moved away to avoid being thrown the Frisbee.
Used water bottle	Martin & Leary (1999)	People find it hard to discredit others' definition of the situation, even when failing to do so may endanger them.	Individuals who had drunk an unpleasant liquid were offered another's used water bottle to drink from. They drank more when the offer implied that they might be worried about sharing the bottle.
Obedience to authority	Milgram (1974)	Individuals obey an authority figure even when the request is an outrageous one that few predict they would obey.	Most people obeyed an experimenter's request to give electrical shock to another person even when the other person was clearly suffering.

(Continued)

Chapter 2: Social Etiquette   *(Continued)*

RESEARCH SUMMARY TABLE 2			
Study	Citation	Key Concept	Key Finding
Prejudice yields to etiquette	LaPiere (1934)	Individuals may act against their true prejudiced feeling rather than act in a way that violates social etiquette.	Individuals reported that they would discriminate against Chinese individuals in their establishments, but when confronted with a Chinese couple requesting accommodation, only one actually discriminated.
Etiquette yields to prejudice	Swim & Hyers (1999)	Individuals may conceal their discomfort about others' prejudice rather than violate social etiquette.	Women confronted with a man's sexist comments typically failed to confront him. Afterward, while watching a videotape of the interaction, they noted that they often thought about confronting him. Observers' ratings of how impolite various responses would be predicted the likelihood that women would use them.

Chapter 3: Conformity

RESEARCH SUMMARY TABLE 3			
Study	Citation	Key Concept	Key Finding
Johnny Rocco case	Schachter (1951)	Individuals with deviant opinions are rejected both in terms of behaviors and ratings.	In a group discussion, those with deviant opinions were rejected by others. Other people stopped talking to them when it was clear that they would not change their opinion; group members also rated them as the least-liked discussion members.
Picking who gets shocks	Freedman & Doob (1968)	Individuals are punished for their deviant opinions.	Group members selected conforming group members to be in studies with the potential to win money and deviating group members to be in studies with the potential to receive electric shocks.
Juan Corona jury case	Villasenor (1977)	Dissenters are bullied into changing their opinions.	In a real-life jury trial, the lone dissenting voter finally changed her vote because of the extreme pressure she felt.
Federal judges' votes	Cross & Tiller (1998)	Even judges may conform to other judges' behaviors.	Real-life data on three judge panels reveal that the political orientation of the other two judges was a strong predictor of the third judge's vote.
Johnson administration cabinet room	Thomson (1968, cited in Janis, 1982)	Dissenters are punished for their deviant opinions and may alter their opinions to be more conforming.	In an analysis of President Johnson's cabinet during the Vietnam War, senior officials who questioned the administration's policy were given disparaging labels. In response, they often softened their criticism.
Law students and "lesbian baiting"	Guinier, Fine, & Balin (1997)	Individuals who act in deviant ways are given disparaging labels to discourage their deviant behavior.	Female law students who spoke up in class were labeled "man-hating lesbians." In response, female students stopped speaking up in class.
Rate busters	Coch & French (1948)	Deviant behavior is discouraged through rejection and punishment.	In a manufacturing plant, those who worked too slowly or too quickly were pressured to fall in line through silent treatment or being called names such as "rate busters."
Street corner society's bowling hierarchy	Whyte (1943)	Individuals are pressured to act in ways that support the prevailing hierarchy, even on dimensions that do not define the hierarchy.	Youth gang members are expected to bowl at their level in their hierarchy. Low-ranking members who bowled very well were harassed until they scored at their appropriate low level.

(Continued)

Chapter 3: Conformity   *(Continued)*

RESEARCH SUMMARY TABLE 3			
Study	Citation	Key Concept	Key Finding
Bennington College study	Newcomb (1943)	Group members are affected by group norms. Those group members most in line with group norms are the most popular.	Conservative women became more liberal when they attended Bennington. The most liberal women were the ones considered most popular; the women who remained conservative were socially isolated.
Sororities and binging	Crandall (1988)	Group members who follow the group norms are considered most popular.	Sorority women friendships were related to the women's levels of binge eating. Those friendship groups that binged at that right level (a high amount in one sorority, a moderate amount in another) were the most popular ones.
Judging lengths of lines	Asch (1955, 1956)	Individuals change their behavior to match others' behavior even without explicit pressure. They censor their true opinions because it is uncomfortable to be different.	In a group of six people, individuals were asked to select which of a group of lines matched another. When the other five reported the wrong answer to this unambiguous task, most participants went along with the others at least some of the time.
Eat lightly norm	Mori, Chaiken, & Pliner (1987)	Individuals conform to cultural norms to appear attractive to other people.	Hungry female participants ate fewer crackers when with a desirable male than with an undesirable male. They altered their behavior to fit with the feminine norm of eating lightly.
Anti-littering norms	Cialdini, Reno, & Kallgren (1991)	Individuals conform to ideals of how one should act.	When individuals saw others either picking up litter or tossing litter into a clean space, they tended to litter less, presumably because these actions reminded them of the anti-littering ideal norm.
Quiet in the library	Aarts & Dijksterhuis (2003)	Conformity to norms may happen automatically without one's awareness.	Individuals who saw a picture of a library and expected to visit a library talked more quietly in an allegedly separate study than those who saw a picture of an empty platform at a railway station or those who saw the library but did not expect to visit it.

Chapter 4: Self-Censorship and the Collective

Study	Citation	Key Concept	Key Finding
RESEARCH SUMMARY TABLE 4			
Smoke-filled room	Latané & Darley (1968)	Pluralistic ignorance may inhibit bystanders from responding when there are other bystanders present.	Bystanders were more likely to intervene in an emergency situation when they were alone than when other bystanders were present.
Transparency of concern	Gilovich, Savitsky, & Medvec (1998)	Individuals believe that their true feelings are transparent even when they are concealing them; they display an illusion of transparency.	Individuals reported being more concerned about another person's actions than they thought that others were concerned about the actions. They also felt that they looked more concerned than others did.
Misperceiving drinking norms	Perkins & Berkowitz (1986)	Pluralistic ignorance exists around college alcohol consumption.	Students reported that their own attitudes about drinking were less permissive than they perceived other students' attitudes to be.
Drinking norms and illusion of transparency	Prentice & Miller (1996)	Individuals believe that their true feelings about comfort with alcohol are transparent even when they are concealing them.	Individuals reported that others were more comfortable with alcohol than they were. They also reported that others could see that they were less comfortable, although others actually did not see their discomfort.
Pro-life and pro-choice groups	Robinson, Keltner, Ward, & Ross (1995)	Group members see outgroup members as more extreme and homogeneous than they are. Additionally, ingroup members see their own group members as more extreme than they are.	Although pro-life and pro-choice individuals do differ in their opinions, a study showed that the differences were not as extreme as the other group or their own group members perceived them to be.
Insulting southerners and northerners	Cohen, Nisbett, Bowdle, & Schwarz (1996)	The persistence of norms may result from widespread misperception about support for the norms.	Southern males believed that their not retaliating against an insult would be perceived as less masculine (although they did not see it as unmanly); northern males did not share this perception.
Support for the culture of honor	Vandello, Cohen, & Ransom (2004)	Individuals misperceive others' support for group norms.	Both southern and northern males reported a low probability that they would punch someone in a bar, but southern males assumed that other males at their university would punch the person.

(Continued)

Chapter 4: Self-Censorship and the Collective   (*Continued*)

RESEARCH SUMMARY TABLE 4			
Study	Citation	Key Concept	Key Finding
Dispelling pluralistic ignorance	Schroeder & Prentice (1998)	Providing information about actual group norms and the principles of pluralistic ignorance may dispel pluralistic ignorance.	Students exposed to actual norms on students' comfort with drinking and information about pluralistic ignorance reported drinking less months after the intervention than those who had been exposed to information about making responsible decisions about drinking.

Chapter 5: Self-Censorship and the Individual

RESEARCH SUMMARY TABLE 5			
Study	Citation	Key Concept	Key Finding
Classroom pluralistic ignorance	Miller & McFarland (1987)	Pluralistic ignorance leaves students feeling inferior.	Students read an incomprehensible article but did not ask questions because they did not want to embarrass themselves; they assumed that others did not ask questions because they knew the information. Students not only did not learn the information in the article, but also felt inferior to their peers.
Health care burnout	Maslach (1982)	Censoring negative feelings may leave one feeling unique and incompetent.	Health care professionals concealed their feelings of anxiety, thus leading them to the erroneous conclusion that they were alone in feeling anxious. As a result, they felt less competent.
Water shortage and not showering	Monin & Norton (2003)	Pluralistic ignorance may leave one assuming that one's own motives are different from, and less noble than, the motivations of others.	Students reported responding to a water shortage by showering less, but they assumed that they were motivated less by community solidarity than other students were.
Keg bans	Prentice & Miller (1993)	Feeling out of step with other group members leaves one feeling deviant from, and unconnected to, the group.	Students who believed they were deviants in supporting a campus keg ban reported that they were less likely to take action on the keg ban, less likely to attend college reunions, and less likely to donate money to the college.
Fear of romantic rejection	Vorauer & Ratner (1996)	Pluralistic ignorance about others' romantic feelings leads individuals not to initiate relationships.	Individuals assumed that their own aloof behavior reflected fear of being romantically rejected whereas others' aloof behavior reflected lack of interest. As a result, they do not initiate relationships.

Chapter 6: Censoring and Expressing Prejudice

RESEARCH SUMMARY TABLE 6			
Study	Citation	Key Concept	Key Finding
Electric shocks and race	Rogers & Prentice-Dunn (1981)	Individuals may censor latent hostility.	Black confederates were given lower-intensity shocks than whites when they were pleasant but higher-intensity shocks than whites when they insulted the white participants.
Blatant and subtle measures of prejudice	McConahay (1986)	Subtle measures more effectively capture prejudices than blatant measures.	Explicit measures to assess prejudice have been updated from blatant to more subtle ones that are better able to capture the range of prejudiced beliefs.
Measuring prejudice with facial expressions	Vanman, Paul, Ito, & Miller (1997)	Individuals' unconscious prejudices leak out in their nonverbal facial expressions.	White participants' facial muscle activity (as measured by facial EMG) was higher in frowning than in smiling muscles when presented with black faces; the opposite pattern was seen with white faces.
Measuring prejudice with voice quality	Weitz (1972)	Voice quality may capture prejudices individuals want to conceal; those who most deny prejudice are most apt to display it through their voice quality.	White participants ostensibly interacting with black partners over an intercom system were less warm than those interacting with white partners. *Less* warm voice quality was associated with *more* positive self-reported attitudes.
Spreading activation theory (SAT)	Collins & Loftus (1975)	SAT is the theoretical basis for implicit measures of prejudice.	When certain concepts were activated, associated concepts were also activated –(e.g., priming *doctor* activates the word *nurse*).
Implicit racial prejudice	Fazio, Jackson, Dunton, & Williams (1995)	Whites hold implicit negative stereotypes about blacks. The stronger these implicit stereotypes, the more behavioral signs of prejudiced whites showed.	After seeing a black face (as compared to a white face) white participants were slower to identify positive adjectives and were quicker to identify negative adjectives. Showing more implicit prejudice also predicted the black experimenter's rating of a particpant as acting less warm.
"Morning" and "night" people's control of stereotypes	Bodenhausen (1990)	It is difficult to control one's expressions of prejudice while cognitively taxed.	People who functioned best in the morning were more likely to find the Hispanic defendant guilty when tested at night, whereas people who functioned best at night were more likely to find the Hispanic defendant guilty when tested in the morning.

(Continued)

Chapter 6: Censoring and Expressing Prejudice   *(Continued)*

RESEARCH SUMMARY TABLE 6			
Study	Citation	Key Concept	Key Finding
Egalitarians' control of stereotypes	Moskowitz, Gollwitzer, Wasel, & Schaal (1999)	Some individuals do not have stereotypes automatically activated but are instead able to control them preconsciously.	Nonegalitarians shown black faces were quicker to pronounce stereotype-relevant than irrelevant words. Egalitarians in the same condition did not pronounce these words quicker.
Counteracting the label "racist"	Fein, Hoshino-Browne, Davies, & Spencer (2002)	Desire to counteract the idea that one is racist may prevent stereotype activation.	Individuals who received feedback that they were racist later showed less stereotype activation than those who did not receive this feedback.
Game of scrabble and race	Frey & Gaertner (1986)	Individuals justify discriminatory behavior by using the stereotyped member's questionable behavior.	White participants helped black and white Scrabble players equally when the game was difficult through no fault of the player. However, they were less helpful to black than white players if the players' struggles were caused by perceived laziness.
Bystander effect and race	Gaertner & Dovidio (1977)	Individuals justify discriminatory behavior by using the ambiguity of the situation.	White participants helped blacks slightly *more* than whites when they believed that they were the only one witnessing the emergency. However, they helped blacks much *less* than whites when they believed others also witnessed the emergency.
Picking movies and race	Batson, Flink, Schoenrade, Fultz, & Pych (1986)	Individuals discriminate more when it is clear that their behavior could be caused by a non-discriminatory motive.	White participants chose to sit next to the black person more when the same movies were playing on two monitors than when different movies were playing on both monitors.
Being called "not racist" as moral credentials	Fein, Hoshino-Browne, Davies, & Spencer (2002)	Individuals who are told that they are not racist (and therefore have gained "moral credentials") are freer to act in ways that could be seen as prejudiced.	Individuals who received feedback that they were not racist were later less likely to pick a weak black candidate over a stronger white candidate.

(Continued)

Chapter 6: Censoring and Expressing Prejudice   *(Continued)*

RESEARCH SUMMARY TABLE 6			
Study	Citation	Key Concept	Key Finding
Nonpre-judiced track record as moral credentials	Monin & Miller (2001)	Individuals who through their previous behavior demonstrated low prejudice are freer to act in ways that could be seen as prejudiced. This seems to result from actual concern with being prejudiced, not just from appearing unprejudiced.	Individuals who were in a condition in which they initially selected a black applicant were more likely in a second task not to recommend a black for a job in a hostile work environment than those who were in a condition in which they initially selected a white applicant. This effect occurred regardless of whether the audience for the second decision knew about the initial selection.
Restaurant dress codes and race	Dutton (1971)	Individuals may show preferential treatment to blacks in order not to appear prejudiced.	In restaurants requiring a tie, black couples were twice as likely as white couples to be seated when the man did not have a tie.

Chapter 7: Censoring and Expressing Irrationality

RESEARCH SUMMARY TABLE 7			
Study	Citation	Key Concept	Key Finding
Chocolate cockroaches	Hsee (1999)	Individuals make choices in which they censor themselves in order to appear rational.	College students chose a more expensive chocolate cockroach over a less expensive chocolate heart.
Psychological study payment	Blount & Bazerman (1996)	Individuals censor their feelings of unfairness in order to make a selection in which they receive the most money.	When unaware of the other option, individuals chose a lower-paying experiment in which everyone was paid the same amount over a higher-paying experiment in which others were being paid more. When choosing between the two options, individuals chose the higher-paying experiment even though they would likely resent the unfair pay.
Job offers and office size	Tversky & Griffin (1991)	Individuals make selections in order to appear rational although they may know that the decision will result in lower psychological well-being.	Individuals were confronted with two jobs, one involving a small office for them (which was similar to an equally qualified other person's office), the other involving a medium office for them (which was smaller than that of an equally qualified other person). Individuals reported that they would choose the job with the larger office although they would be happier with the fairer office allocation.
MBA job offers and salaries	Bazerman, Schroth, Shah, Diekmann, & Tensbrunsel (1994)	Individuals censor feelings of procedural justice in order to give the appearance of maximizing salary considerations.	When the jobs were presented one at a time, individuals were more likely to select the job in which they were treated with more respect than the job with less respect and more money. Asked to choose between the two jobs, they selected money over respect.

(Continued)

Chapter 7: Censoring and Expressing Irrationality   *(Continued)*

RESEARCH SUMMARY TABLE 7			
Study	Citation	Key Concept	Key Finding
Fairness & litigation	Tyler, Huo, & Lind (1999)	Individuals will make a decision that will bring them less satisfaction because it is the rational choice.	Individuals' likelihood to sue over lost work depended on how much money they expected to make. Their satisfaction after the case was more highly predicted by how fairly they perceived they were treated than how much money they made.
Baby pacifier study	Brown (1970)	Individuals censor their feelings of embarrassment in order to appear rational.	Individuals would receive more money for giving a live presentation about a baby pacifier than a written one. When their audience did not know of the payment schedule, participants chose the written description. But when the audience knew, participants chose the embarrassing live presentation for which they received more money.
Choosing college courses	Wilson & Schooler (1991)	Thinking about the reasons for their behavior may shift people toward more "rational" and less satisfying choices.	Individuals asked to select college courses based their decisions in large part on other students' evaluations. However, when asked to think about and rate each of the possible reasons for selecting a course, participants used more legitimate reasons, such as course format or content.
National election study	Sears & Funk (1990)	Individuals emphasize self-interest when explaining their behavior even though other less seemingly rational reasons may account for it.	Individuals' voting behavior was generally found to be largely unrelated to how much better or worse off they reported being compared to four years before. But when they are asked this question in exit polls, there is a strong correlation, suggesting that people do not want to appear to be acting against their economic self-interest.

(Continued)

Chapter 7: Censoring and Expressing Irrationality   (Continued)

	RESEARCH SUMMARY TABLE 7		
Study	Citation	Key Concept	Key Finding
Americans are helpful	Wuthnow (1991)	People may conceal their compassion under the guise of self-interest.	Although many Americans engage in various acts of compassion and kindness, they emphasize that the behaviors are motivated by more practical or instrumental reasons.
Lying about a boring task	Festinger & Carlsmith (1959)	People may use self-interest to justify morally questionable behavior.	Individuals paid $20 to lie to someone else did not believe their lie, but those paid only $1 changed their opinion to be more in line with the lie they told. Presumably receiving $20 justified lying.
Proofreading text	Hsee (1995)	Individuals are freer to act on their true (albeit less rational) choices if the reason for their choice is ambiguous.	When it was clear that reading boring furniture ads would yield higher pay than reading more interesting personal ads, participants read more furniture ads. When it was not entirely clear, although probable, that reading furniture ads would be more profitable, participants chose to read more personal ads.
Exchange fiction	Holmes, Miller, & Lerner (2001)	Incentives may serve to provide a justification for helping rather than actually motivate helping.	Individuals faced with a high-need situation gave more when offered an incentive in exchange for helping than when offered no incentive. Those faced with a low-need situation were unaffected by the incentive.
Learning economic theory	Frank, Gilovich, & Regan (1993)	Those who have had an economics course act more in line with their self-interest.	Students taking economic courses (particularly those taught by experts in theories emphasizing self-interest) came to believe that acting in a self-interested way was the rational and appropriate way to act.

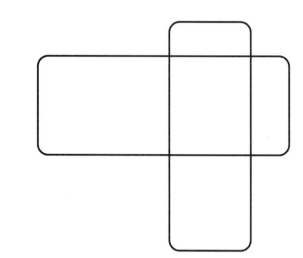

References

Aarts, H., & Dijksterhuis, A. (2003). The silence of the library: Environment, situational norm, and social behavior. *Journal of Personality and Social Psychology, 84,* 18–28.

Allport, F. H. (1924). *Social psychology.* Boston, MA: Houghton Mifflin.

Allport, G. W. (1954). *The nature of prejudice.* Reading, MA: Addison-Wesley.

Asch, S. E. (1955). Opinions and social pressure. *Scientific American, 193,* 31–55.

Asch, S. E. (1956). Studies of independence and conformity: A minority of one against a unanimous majority. *Psychological Monographs, 7,* No. 9 (Whole No. 416).

Batson, C. D., Flink, C. H., Schoenrade, P. A., Fultz, J., & Pych, V. (1986). Religious orientation and overt versus covert racial prejudice. *Journal of Personality and Social Psychology, 50,* 175–181.

Batson, C. D., Thompson, E. R., Seuferling, G., Whitney, H., & Strongman, J. (1999). Moral hypocrisy: Appearing moral to oneself without being so. *Journal of Personality and Social Psychology, 77,* 525–537.

Baumeister, R. F., & Leary, M. R. (1995). The need to belong: Desire for interpersonal attachments as a fundamental human motivation. *Psychological Bulletin, 117,* 497–529.

Bazerman, M. H., Schroth, H. A., Shah, P. P., Diekmann, K. A. & Tenbrunsel, A. E. (1994). The inconsistent role of comparison others and procedural justice in reactions to hypothetical job descriptions: Implications for job acceptance decisions. *Organizational Behavior and Human Decision Processes, 60,* 326–352.

Benaquisto, L., & Freed, P. J. (1996). The myth of inmate lawlessness: The perceived contradiction between self and other in inmates' support for criminal justice sanctioning norms. *Law & Society Review, 30,* 489–511.

Berkowitz, A. D., & Perkins, H. W. (1986). Problem drinking among college students: A review of recent research. *Journal of American College Health, 35,* 21–28.

Bernstein, W. M., Stephenson, B. O., Snyder, M. L., & Wicklund, R. A. (1983). Causal ambiguity and heterosexual affiliation. *Journal of Experimental Social Psychology, 19,* 78–92.

Biernat, M., & Crandall, C. S. (1999). Racial attitudes. In J. Robinson, P. R. Shaver, & L. S. Wrightsman (Eds.), *Measures of political attitudes* (pp. 297–411). San Diego, CA: Academic Press.

Blair, I. V. (2002). The malleability of automatic stereotypes and prejudice. *Personality and Social Psychology Review, 6,* 242–261.

Blount, S., & Bazerman, M. H. (1996). The inconsistent evaluation of absolute versus comparative payoffs in labor supply and bargaining. *Journal of Economic Behavior and Organization, 30,* 227–240.

Bodenhausen, G. V. (1990). Stereotypes as judgmental heuristics: Evidence of circadian variation in discrimination. *Psychological Science, 1,* 319–322.

Bodenhausen, G. V., Sheppard, L. A., & Kramer, G. F. (1994). Negative affect and social judgment: The differential impact of anger and sadness. *European Journal of Social Psychology, 24,* 45–62.

Brown, B. R. (1970). Face-saving following experimentally induced embarrassment. *Journal of Experimental Social Psychology, 6,* 255–271.

Brunk, G. G. (1980). The impact of rational participation models on voting attitudes. *Public Choice, 35,* 549–564.

Bryan, A. D., Aiken, L. S., & West, S. G. (1999). The impact of a male proposing condom use on perceptions of an initial sexual encounter. *Personality and Social Psychology Bulletin, 25,* 275–286.

Bushman, B. J. (1988). The effects of apparel on compliance: A field experiment with a female authority figure. *Personality and Social Psychology Bulletin, 14,* 459–467.

Cialdini, R. B. (2001). *Influence: Science and practice* (4th ed.). Boston: Allyn & Bacon.

Cialdini, R. B., Reno, R. R., & Kallgren, C. A. (1991). A focus theory of normative conduct: A theoretical refinement and re-evaluation of the role of norms in human behavior. In M. P. Zanna (Ed.), *Advances in experimental social psychology* (Vol. 24, pp. 201–234). San Diego, CA: Academic Press.

Chaiken, S., & Pliner, P. (1987). Women, but not men, are what they eat: The effect of meal size and gender on perceived femininity and masculinity. *Personality and Social Psychology Bulletin, 13,* 166–176.

Chartrand, T. L., & Bargh, J. A. (1999). The chameleon effect: The perception-behavior link and social interaction. *Journal of Personality and Social Psychology, 76,* 983–910.

Clymer, A. (1989, 12 November). Election Day shows what the opinion polls can't do. *New York Times,* 14.

Coch, L., & French, J. R. P., Jr. (1948). Overcoming resistance to change. *Human Relations, 11,* 41–53.

Cohen, D., Nisbett, R. E., Bowdle, B. F., & Schwarz, N. (1996). Insult, aggression, and the southern culture of honor: An "experimental ethnography." *Journal of Personality and Social Psychology, 70,* 945–960.

Cohen, L. L., & Shotland, R. L. (1996). Timing of first sexual intercourse in a relationship: Expectations, experiences, and perceptions of others. *Journal of Sex Research, 33,* 291–299.

Collins, A. M., & Loftus, E. F. (1975). A spreading-activation theory of semantic processing. *Psychological Review, 82,* 407–428.

Costrich, N., Feinstein, J., Kidder, L., Marecek, J., & Pascal, L. (1975). When stereotypes hurt: Three studies of penalties for sex-role reversals. *Journal of Experimental Social Psychology, 11,* 520–530.

Crandall, C. S. (1988). Social contagion of binge eating. *Journal of Personality and Social Psychology, 55,* 588–598.

Crandall, C. S., Eshleman, A., & O'Brien, L. (2002). Social norms and the expression and suppression of prejudice: The struggle for internalization. *Journal of Personality and Social Psychology, 82*, 359–378.

Crosby, F., Bromley, S., & Saxe, L. (1980). Recent unobtrusive studies of Black and White discrimination and prejudice: A literature review. *Psychological Bulletin, 87*, 546–563.

Cross, F., & Tiller, E. (1998). Judicial partisanship and obedience to legal doctrine. *Yale Law Journal, 107*, 2155–2176.

Darley, J. M., & Latané, B. (1970). Norms and normative behavior: Field studies of social interdependence. In J. Macaulay & L. Berkowitz (Eds.), *Altruism and helping behavior* (pp. 83–101). New York: Academic Press.

De Paulo, B. M., & Friedman, H. S. (1998). Nonverbal communication. In D. T. Gilbert, S. T. Fiske, & G. Lindzey (Eds.), *The handbook of social psychology* (4th ed., Vol. 2, pp. 3–40). New York: McGraw-Hill.

De Tocqueville, A. (1955/1856). *The old regime and the French Revolution.* S. Gilbert (Trans.). New York: Doubleday/Anchor.

De Tocqueville, A. (1969/1835). *Democracy in America.* J. P. Mayer (Ed.), G. Lawrence (Trans.). Garden City, NY: Anchor Books.

Deutsch, M. (1973). *The resolution of conflict: Constructive and destructive processes.* New Haven, CT: Yale University Press.

Deutsch, M., & Gerard, H. G. (1955). A study of normative and informational social influence upon individual judgment. *Journal of Abnormal and Social Psychology, 51*, 629–636.

Devine, P. G. (1989). Stereotyping and prejudice: Their automatic and controlled components. *Journal of Personality and Social Psychology, 56*, 5–18.

Dovidio, J. F., Kawakami, K., Johnson, B., & Howard, A. (1997). On the nature of prejudice: Automatic and controlled processes. *Journal of Experimental Social Psychology, 33*, 510–540.

Duncan, B. L. (1976). Differential social perception and attribution of intergroup violence: Testing the lower limits of stereotyping of Blacks. *Journal of Personality and Social Psychology, 34*, 590–598.

Dutton, D. G. (1971). Reactions of restaurateurs to Blacks and Whites violating restaurant dress requirements. *Canadian Journal of Behavioural Science, 3*, 298–302.

Dutton, D. G. (1973). Reverse discrimination: The relationship of amount of perceived discrimination toward a minority group in the behavior of majority group members. *Canadian Journal of Behavioural Science, 5*, 34–45.

Dutton, D. G., & Lake, R. A. (1973). Threat of own prejudice and reverse discrimination in interracial situations. *Journal of Personality and Social Psychology, 28*, 94–100.

Eberhardt, J. L., Goff, P. A., Purdie, V. J., & Davies, P. G. (2004). Seeing Black: Race, crime, and visual processing. *Journal of Personality and Social Psychology, 87*, 876–893.

Emerson, J. P. (1970). Nothing unusual is happening. In T. Shibutani (Ed.), *Human nature and collective behavior: Papers in honor of Herbert Blumer* (pp. 208–222). Englewood Cliffs, NJ: Prentice-Hall.

Eyer, D. (1996). *Mother guilt: How our culture blames mothers for what's wrong with society.* New York: Times Books.

Fazio, R. H., Jackson, J. R., Dunton, B. C., & Williams, C. J. (1995). Variability in automatic activation as an unobtrusive measure of racial attitudes: A bona fide pipeline? *Journal of Personality and Social Psychology, 69*, 1013–1027.

Fazio, R. H., & Towles-Schwen, T. (1999). The MODE model of attitude-behavior processes. In S. Chaiken & Y. Trope (Eds.), *Dual-process theories in social psychology* (pp. 97–116). New York: Guilford.

Fein, S., Hoshino-Browne, E., Davies, P. G., & Spencer, S. J. (2002). Self-image maintenance goals and sociocultural norms and motivated social perception. In S. J. Spencer, M. P. Zanna, & J. M. Olson (Eds.), *Motivated social perception: The Ontario Symposium* (Vol. 9, pp 21–44). Mahwah, NJ: Erlbaum.

Festinger, L., & Carlsmith, J. M. (1959). Cognitive consequences of forced compliance. *Journal of Abnormal and Social Psychology, 58,* 203–210.

Fields, J. M., & Schuman, H. (1976). Public beliefs and the beliefs of the public. *Public Opinion Quarterly, 40,* 427–448.

Finkel, S. K., Guterbock, T. M., & Borg, M. J. (1991). Race of interviewer effects in a preelection poll. *Public Opinion Quarterly, 55,* 313–330.

Fiske, S. T. (1998). Stereotyping, prejudice, and discrimination. In D. T. Gilbert, S. T. Fiske, & G. Lindsey (Eds.), *Handbook of social psychology* (4th ed., Vol. 2, pp. 357–411). New York: McGraw-Hill.

Frank, R. H., Gilovich, T., & Regan, D. T. (1993). Does studying economics inhibit cooperation? *Journal of Economic Perspectives, 7,* 159–171.

Freedman, J. L., & Doob, A. N. (1968). *Deviancy: The psychology of being different.* New York: Academic Press.

Friedman, L. S., Lichtenstein, E., & Biglan, A. (1985). Smoking onset among teens: An empirical analysis of initial situations. *Addictive Behaviors, 10,* 1–13.

Frey, D., & Gaertner, S. L. (1986). Helping and the avoidance of inappropriate interpersonal behavior: A strategy that can perpetuate a non-prejudicial self-image. *Journal of Personality and Social Psychology, 50,* 1083–1090.

Gaertner, S. L., & Bickman, L. (1971). Effects of race on elicitation of helping behavior: The wrong number technique. *Journal of Personality and Social Psychology, 20,* 218–222.

Gaertner, S. L., & Dovidio, J. F. (1977). The subtlety of White racism, arousal, and helping behavior. *Journal of Personality and Social Psychology, 35,* 691–707.

Gaertner, S. L., & Dovidio, J. F. (1986). The aversive form of racism. In J. F. Dovidio and S. L. Gaertner (Eds.), *Prejudice, discrimination, and racism* (pp. 61–90). Orlando, FL: Academic Press.

Gilovich, T., Savitsky, K., & Medvec, V. H. (1998). The illusion of transparency: Biased assessments of others' ability to read one's emotional states. *Journal of Personality and Social Psychology, 75,* 332–346.

Goffman, E. (1959). *The presentation of self in everyday life.* New York: Doubleday-Anchor Books.

Goffman, E. (1971) *Relations in public.* New York: Harper & Row.

Gold, R. S., Skinner, M. J., Grant, P. J., & Plummer, D. C. (1991). Situational factors and thought processes associated with unprotected intercourse in gay men. *Psychology and Health, 5,* 259–278.

Green, D. P., & Cowden, J. A. (1992). Who protests: Self-interest and White opposition to busing. *Journal of Politics, 54,* 471–496.

Greenwald, A. G., & Banaji, M. R. (1995) Implicit social cognition: Attitudes, self-esteem, and stereotypes. *Psychological Review, 102,* 4–27.

Greenwald, A. G., McGhee, D. E., & Schwartz, J. K. (1998). Measuring individual differences in implicit cognition: The Implicit Attitude Test. *Journal of Personality and Social Psychology, 74,* 1464–1480.

Gross, S. R., & Ellsworth, P. C. (2003). Second thoughts: American's views on the death penalty at the turn of the century. In S. P. Garvey (Ed.), *Beyond repair? America's death penalty* (pp. 7–57). Durham, NC: Duke University Press.

Guinier, L., Fine, M., & Balin, J. (1997). *Becoming gentlemen.* Boston, MA: Beacon Press.

Hadaway, C. K., Marler, P. L., & Chaves, M. (1993). What the polls don't show: A closer look at U.S. church attendance. *American Sociological Review, 56,* 741–752.

Haines, M. P., & Spear, S. F. (1996). Changing perception of the norm: A strategy to decrease binge drinking among college students. *Journal of American College Health, 45(3),* 134–140.

Harper, C. R., Kidera, G. J., & Cullen, J. F. (1971). Study of simulated airline pilot incapacitation: Phase II, subtle or partial loss of function. *Aerospace Medicine, 42,* 946–948.

Helmreich, R. L. (1997). Managing human error in aviation. *Scientific American,* May, 62–67.

Henry, P. J., & Sears, D. O. (2002). The symbolic racism 2000 scale. *Political Psychology, 23,* 253–283.

Hinckley, E. D. (1932). The influence of individual opinion on construction of an attitude scale. *Journal of Social Psychology, 3,* 283–296.

Hodson, G., Dovidio, J. F., & Gaertner, S. L. (2002). Processes in racial discrimination: Differential weighting of conflicting information. *Personality and Social Psychology Bulletin, 28,* 460–471.

Holmes, J. G., Miller, D. T., & Lerner, M. J. (2001). Committing altruism under the cloak of self-interest: The exchange fiction. *Journal of Experimental Social Psychology, 38,* 144–151.

Hsee, C. K. (1995). Elastic justification: How tempting but task-irrelevant factors influence decisions. *Organizational Behavior and Human Decision Processes, 62,* 330–337.

Hsee, C. K. (1999). Value-seeking and prediction-decision inconsistency: Why don't people take what they predict they'll like most? *Psychonomic Bulletin and Review, 6,* 555–561.

Hsee, C. K., Zhang, J., Yu, F., & Xi, Y. (2003). Lay rationalism and inconsistency between predicted experience and decision. *Journal of Behavioral Decision Making, 16,* 257–272.

Hunter, S. M., Vizelberg, I. A., & Berenson, G. S. (1991). Identifying mechanisms of adoption of tobacco and alcohol use among youth: The Bogalusa Heart Study. *Social Networks, 13,* 91–104.

Hyman, H. H., & Sheatsley, P. B. (1956). Attitudes and desegregation. *Scientific American, 195(6),* 35–39.

Janis, I. (1982). *Victims of groupthink: A psychological study of foreign-policy decisions and fiascoes* (Rev. ed.), Boston, MA: Houghton Mifflin.

Jones, E. E., Farina, A., Hastorf, A. H., Markus, H., Miller, D. T., Scott, R. A., & French, R. S. (1984). *Social stigma: The psychology of marked relationships.* New York: W. H. Freeman.

Jones, J. M. (1997). *Prejudice and racism.* (2nd ed.). New York: McGraw-Hill.

Kandel, D. B. (1980). Drug and drinking behavior among youth. *Annual Review of Sociology, 6,* 235–285.

Katz, D., & Schanck, R. L. (1938). *Social psychology.* New York: John Wiley & Sons.

Katz, I., Hass, R. G., & Wackenhut, J. (1986). Racial ambivalence, value duality, and behavior. In J. F. Dovidio and S. L. Gaertner (Eds.). *Prejudice, discrimination, and racism* (pp. 35–59). Orlando, FL: Academic Press.

Kinder, D. R. (1998). Opinion and action in the realm of politics. In D. T. Gilbert, S. T. Fiske, & G. Lindzey (Eds.) *Handbook of Social Psychology,* Vol. 2, pp. 778–867. New York: McGraw-Hill.

Kinder, D. R., & Kiewiet, D. R. (1981). Sociotropic politics: The American case. *British Journal of Political Science, 11,* 129–161.

Kinsey, A. C., Pomeroy, W. B., & Martin, C. E. (1948). *Sexual behavior in the human male.* Philadelphia, PA: Saunders.

Kitts, J. A. (2003). Egocentric bias or information management? Selective disclosure and the social roots of norm misperception. *Social Psychology Quarterly, 66,* 222–238.

Klassen, A. D., Williams, C. J., & Levitt, E. E. (1989). *Sex and morality in the U.S.: An empirical inquiry under the auspices of the Kinsey Institute.* Wesleyan, CT: Wesleyan University Press.

Kunda, Z. (1999). *Social cognition: Making sense of people.* Cambridge: MIT Press.

Kunda, Z., & Sinclair, L. (1999). Motivated reasoning with stereotypes: Activation, application, and inhibition. *Psychological Inquiry, 10,* 12–22.

Kunda, Z., & Spencer, S. J. (2003). When do stereotypes come to mind and when do they color judgment? A goal-based theory of stereotype activation and application. *Psychological Bulletin, 129,* 522–544.

Kuran, T. (1995). *Private truths, public lies.* Cambridge, MA: Harvard University Press.

Lambert, T. A., Kahn, A. S., & Apple, K. J. (2003). Pluralistic ignorance and hooking up. *Journal of Sex Research. 40,* 129–133.

LaPiere, R. T. (1934). Attitudes vs. actions. *Social Forces, 13,* 230–237.

Latané, B., & Darley, J. M. (1968). Group inhibition of bystander intervention. *Journal of Personality and Social Psychology, 10,* 215–221.

Latané, B., & Darley, J. M. (1970). *The unresponsive bystander: Why doesn't he help?* New York: Appelton Century Crofts.

Levine, J. M. (1989). Reaction to opinion deviance in small groups. In P. B. Paulus (Ed.), *The psychology of group influence* (2nd ed., pp.187–231). Hillsdale, NJ: Erlbaum.

Levine, R. (2003). *The power of persuasion.* Hoboken, NJ: John Wiley & Sons.

Linde, C. (1988). The quantitative study of communicative success: Politeness and accidents in aviation discourse. *Language and Society, 17,* 375–399.

Linz, D., Donnerstein, E., Land, K. C., McCall, P. L., Scott, J., Shafer, B. J., Klein, L. J., & Lance, L. (1991). Estimating community standards: The use of social science evidence in an obscenity prosecution. *Public Opinion Quarterly, 55,* 80–112.

Lowery, B. S., Hardin, C. D., & Sinclair, S. (2001). Social influence effects on automatic racial prejudice. *Journal of Personality and Social Psychology, 81,* 842–855.

Luo, M. (2004, 14 September). Excuse me, may I have your seat? *New York Times, 22.*

Markus, H. R., & Wurf, E. (1987). The dynamic self-concept: A social psychological perspective. *Annual Review of Psychology, 38,* 299–337.

Martin, K. A., & Leary, M. R. (1999). Would you drink after a stranger? The influence of self-presentational motives on willingness to take a health risk. *Personality and Social Psychology Bulletin, 25,* 1092–1100.

Maslach, C. (1982). *Burnout: The cost of caring.* Englewood Cliffs, NJ: Prentice Hall.

McConahay, J. B. (1986). Modern racism, ambivalence, and the modern racism scale. In J. F. Dovidio & S. L. Gaertner (Eds.), *Prejudice, discrimination, and racism* (pp. 91–126). Orlando, FL: Academic Press.

McConnell, A. R., & Leibold, J. M. (2001). Relations between the implicit association test, discriminatory behavior, and explicit measures of racial attitudes. *Journal of Experimental Social Psychology, 37,* 435–442.

McFarland, C., & Miller, D. T. (1990). Judgments of self-other similarity: Just like other people only more so. *Personality and Social Psychology Bulletin, 16,* 475–484.

Meyer, D. E., & Schvaneveldt, R. W. (1971). Facilitation in recognizing pairs of words: Evidence of a dependence between retrieval operations. *Journal of Experimental Psychology, 90,* 227–234.

Milgram, S. (1974). *Obedience to authority.* New York: Harper & Row.

Milgram S., & Sabini, J. (1978). On maintaining urban norms: A field experiment in the subway. In A. Baum, J. E. Singer, & S. Valins (Eds.). *Advances in environmental psychology* (Vol. 1, pp. 31–40). Hillsdale, NJ: Erlbaum.

Miller, D. T. (2001). Disrespect and the experience of injustice. *Annual Review of Psychology, 52,* 527–553.

Miller, D. T., & McFarland, C. (1987). Pluralistic ignorance: When similarity is interpreted as dissimilarity. *Journal of Personality and Social Psychology, 53,* 298–305.

Miller, D. T., & McFarland, C. (1991). When social comparison goes awry: The case of pluralistic ignorance. In J. Suls and T. A. Wills (Eds.), *Social comparison: Contemporary theory and research* (pp. 287–313). Hillsdale, NJ: Erlbaum.

Miller, D.T., & Prentice, D. A. (1994). Collective errors and errors about the collective. *Personality and Social Psychology Bulletin, 20,* 541–550.

Miller, D. T., & Ratner, R. K. (1998). The disparity between the actual and assumed power of self-interest. *Journal of Personality and Social Psychology, 74,* 53–62.

Monin, B., & Miller, D. T. (2001). Moral credentials and the expression of prejudice. *Journal of Personality and Social Psychology, 81,* 5–16.

Monin, B., & Norton, M. I. (2003). Perceptions of fluid consensus: Uniqueness bias, false consensus, false polarization, and pluralistic ignorance in a water conservation crisis. *Personality and Social Psychology Bulletin, 29,* 559–567.

Moore, M. T., & Cauchon, D. (2002, 11 September). Delay meant death on 9/11. *USA Today, 3.*

Mori, D., Chaiken, S., & Pliner, P. (1987). "Eating lightly" and the self-presentation of femininity. *Journal of Personality and Social Psychology, 53,* 693–702.

Morier, D., & Seroy, C. (1994). The effect of interpersonal expectancies on men's self-presentation of gender role attitudes to women. *Sex Roles, 31,* 493–504.

Moskowitz, G. B., Gollwitzer, P. M., Wasel, W., & Schaal, B. (1999). Preconscious control of stereotype activation through chronic egalitarian goals. *Journal of Personality and Social Psychology 77,* 167–184.

Myrdal, G. (1944). *An American Dilemma: The Negro problem and modern democracy.* New York: Harper.

Nelson, T. D. (2002). *The psychology of prejudice.* Boston, MA: Allyn & Bacon.

Newcomb, T. M. (1943). *Personality and social change.* New York: Dryden.

Nisbett, R. E., & Cohen, D. (1996). *Culture of honor.* Boulder, CO: Westview Press.

O'Gorman, H. J. (1986). The discovery of pluralistic ignorance: An ironic lesson. *Journal of the History of the Behavioral Sciences, 22,* 333–347.

Payne, B. K. (2001). Prejudice and perception: The role of automatic and controlled processes in misperceiving a weapon. *Journal of Personality and Social Psychology, 81,* 181–192.

Perkins, H. W. (1985). Religious traditions, parents, and peers as determinants of alcohol and drug use among college students. *Review of Religious Research, 27,* 15–31.

Perkins, H. W., & Berkowitz, A. D. (1986). Perceiving the community norms of alcohol use among students: Some research implications for campus alcohol education programming. *International Journal of Addictions, 21,* 15–31.

Pettigrew, T. F., & Meertens, R. W. (1995). Subtle and blatant prejudice in Western Europe. *European Journal of Social Psychology, 25,* 57–75.

Prentice, D. A., & Carranza, E. (2004). Sustaining cultural beliefs in the face of violation: The case of gender stereotypes. In M. Schaller & C. Crandall (Eds.), *The psychological foundations of culture* (pp. 259–280). Mahwah, NJ: Erlbaum.

Prentice, D. A., & Miller, D. T. (1993). Pluralistic ignorance and alcohol use on campus: Some consequences of misperceiving the social norm. *Journal of Personality and Social Psychology, 64,* 243–256.

Prentice, D. A., & Miller, D. T. (1996). Pluralistic ignorance and the perpetuation of social norms of unwitting actors. In M. P. Zanna (Ed.), *Advances in experimental social psychology* (Vol. 22, pp.161–209). San Diego, CA: Academic Press.

Prentice, D. A., & Miller, D. T. (2002). The emergence of homegrown stereotypes. *American Psychologist, 57,* 352–359.

Ratner, R. K., & Miller, D. T. (2001). The norm of self-interest and its effects on social action. *Journal of Personality and Social Psychology, 81,* 5–16.

Robinson, C. E. (1932). *Straw votes.* New York: Columbia University Press.

Robinson, R. J., Keltner, D., Ward, A., & Ross, L. (1995). Actual versus assumed differences in construal: "Naïve realism" in intergroup perception and conflict. *Journal of Personality and Social Psychology, 68,* 404–417.

Rogers, R. W., & Prentice-Dunn, S. (1981). Deindividuation and anger-mediated interracial aggression: Unmasking regressive racism. *Journal of Personality and Social Psychology, 41,* 63–73.

Ross, L., & Nisbett, R. E. (1991). *The person and the situation: Perspectives of social psychology.* New York: McGraw-Hill.

Ross, L., & Ward, A. (1996). Naïve realism: Implication for misunderstanding and divergent perceptions of fairness and bias. In T. Brown, E. Reed, & E. Turiel (Eds.), *Value and knowledge* (pp. 103–135). Hillsdale, NJ: Erlbaum.

Rozin, P., & Fallon, A. E. (1987). A perspective on disgust. *Psychological Review, 94,* 23–41.

Sabini, J., & Silver, M. (1982). *Moralities of everyday life.* New York: Oxford University Press.

Sagar, H. A., & Schofield, J. W. (1980). Racial and behavioral cues in black and white children's perceptions of ambiguously aggressive acts. *Journal of Personality and Social Psychology, 39,* 590–598.

Sanderson, C. A., Darley, J. M., & Messinger, C. S. (2002). "I'm not as thin as you think I am": The development and consequences of feeling discrepant from the thinness norm. *Personality and Social Psychology Bulletin, 28,* 172–183.

Schachter, S. (1951). Deviation, rejection, and communication. *Journal of Abnormal and Social Psychology, 46,* 190–207.

Schroeder, C. M., & Prentice, D. A. (1998). Dispelling pluralistic ignorance to reduce excessive alcohol use among college students. *Journal of Applied Social Psychology, 28,* 2150–2180.

Schuman, H., Steeh, C., Bobo, L., & Krysan, M. (1997). *Racial attitudes in America: Trends and interpretations*. Cambridge, MA: Harvard University Press. (2002 data available at http://tigger.cc.uic.edu/~krysan/racialattitudes.htm.)

Sears, D. O., & Funk, C. L. (1990). Self-interest in Americans' political opinions. In J. J. Mansbridge (Ed.), *Beyond self-interest* (pp. 147–170). Chicago: University of Chicago Press.

Sears, D. O., & Lau, R. R. (1983). Indicating apparently self-interested political preferences. *American Journal of Political Science, 27,* 223–252.

Shamir, J., & Shamir, M. (1997). Pluralistic ignorance across issues and over time. *Public Opinion Quarterly, 61,* 227–260.

Shweder, R. A. (1982). Beyond self-constructed knowledge: The study of culture and morality. *Merrill-Palmer Quarterly, 28,* 41–69.

Smith, E. R., & Mackie, D. M. (2000). *Social psychology.* Philadelphia, PA: Psychology Press.

Snyder, M. L., Kleck, R. E., Strenta, A., & Mentzer, S. J. (1979). Avoidance of the handicapped: An attributional ambiguity analysis. *Journal of Personality and Social Psychology, 37,* 2297–2306.

Steele, C. M. (1997). A threat in the air: How stereotypes shape intellectual identity and performance. *American Psychologist, 52,* 13–29.

Stein, R. M. (1990). Economic voting for governor and U.S. Senator: The electoral consequences of federalism. *Journal of Politics, 52,* 29–53.

Sunstein, C.R. (2003). *Why societies need dissent.* Cambridge MA: Harvard University Press.

Swim, J. K., & Hyers, L. (1999). Excuse me—What did you just say?! Women's public and private responses to sexist remarks. *Journal of Experimental Social Psychology, 35,* 68–88.

Thomson, J. G., Jr. (1968, April). How could Viet Nam happen? An autopsy. *The Atlantic Monthly,* pp. 47–53.

Toch, H., & Klofas, J. (1984). Pluralistic ignorance, revisited. In G. M. Stephenson & J. H. Davis (Eds.), *Progress in applied social psychology* (Vol. 2, pp. 129–159). New York: Wiley.

Tversky, A., & Griffin, D. (1991). Endowment and contrast in judgments of well-being. In F. Strack, M. Argyle, & N. Schwarz (Eds.), *Subjective well-being: An interdisciplinary perspective* (Vol. 21, pp. 101–118). Oxford, England: Pergamon Press.

Tyler, T. R., & Lind, E. A. (1992). A relational model of authority in groups. In M. P. Zanna (Ed.). *Advances in experimental social psychology* (Vol. 25, pp. 115–192). New York: Academic Press.

Tyler, T. R., Huo, Y. J., & Lind, E. A. (1999). The two psychologies of conflict resolution: Differing antecedents of pre-experience choices and post-experience evaluations. *Group Processes and Intergroup Relations, 2,* 99–118.

Van Boven, L. (2000). Pluralistic ignorance and political correctness: The case of affirmative action. *Political Psychology, 21,* 267–276.

Vandello, J. A., & Cohen, D. (2004). When believing is seeing: Sustaining norms of violence in cultures of honor. In M. Schaller & C. Crandall (Eds.), *Psychological foundations of culture* (pp.281–304). Mahwah, NJ: Erlbaum.

Vandello, J. A., Cohen, D., & Ransom, S. (2004). Norm extension and beliefs about male aggression. Unpublished manuscript.

Vanman, E. J., Paul, B. Y., Ito, T. A., & Miller, N. (1997). The modern face of prejudice and structural features that moderate the effect of cooperation on affect. *Journal of Personality and Social Psychology, 73,* 941–959.

Vidmar, N., & Ellsworth, P. (1974). Public opinion and the death penalty. *Stanford Law Review, 26,* 1245–1270.

Villasenor, V. (1977). *Jury: The people vs. Juan Corona.* Boston, MA: Little Brown.

Von Hippel, W., Sekaquaptewa, D., & Vargas, P. (1995). On the role of encoding processes in stereotype maintenance. In M. P. Zanna (Ed.), *Advances in experimental social psychology* (Vol. 27, pp. 177–254), New York: Academic Press.

Vorauer, J. D. (2001). The other side of the story: Transparency estimation in social interaction. In G. B. Moskowitz (Ed.), *Cognitive social psychology: The Princeton symposium on the legacy and future of social cognition* (pp. 261–276). Mahwah, NJ: Erlbaum.

Vorauer, J. D., & Miller, D. T. (1997). Failure to recognize the effect of implicit social influence on the presentation of self. *Journal of Personality and Social Psychology, 73,* 281–295.

Vorauer, J. D., & Ratner, R. K. (1996). Who's going to make the first move? Pluralistic ignorance as an impediment to relationship formation. *Journal of Social and Personal Relationships, 12,* 483–506.

Weitz, S. (1972). Attitude, voice, and behavior: A repressed affect model of interracial interaction. *Journal of Personality and Social Psychology, 24,* 14–21.

Whyte, W. F. (1943). *Street corner society: The social structure of an Italian slum.* Chicago, IL: University of Chicago Press.

Wilson, T. D., & Schooler, J. W. (1991). Thinking too much: Introspection can reduce the quality of preferences and decisions. *Journal of Personality and Social Psychology, 60,* 181–192.

Wuthnow, R. (1991). *Acts of compassion.* Princeton, NJ: Princeton University Press.

Zanna, M. P., & Pack, S. J. (1975). On the self-fulfilling nature of apparent sex-differences in behavior. *Journal of Experimental Social Psychology, 11,* 583–591.

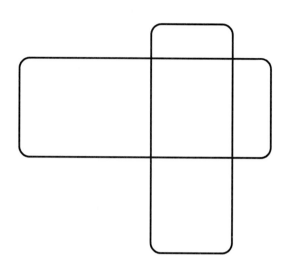

Indexes

Name Index

Subject Index

TO THE OWNER OF THIS BOOK:

I hope that you have found *An Invitation to Social Psychology: Expressing and Censoring the Self* useful. So that this book can be improved in a future edition, would you take the time to complete this sheet and return it? Thank You.

School and address: _____

_____

Department: _____

Instructor's name: _____

1. What I like most about this book is: _____

_____

_____

2. What I like least about this book is: _____

_____

_____

3. My general reaction to this book is: _____

_____

_____

4. The name of the course in which I used this book is: _____

_____

5. Were all of the chapters of the book assigned for you to read?: _____

   If not, which ones weren't? _____

6. In the space below, or on a separate sheet of paper, please write specific suggestions for improving this book and anything else you'd care to share about your experience in using this book.

_____

_____

FOLD HERE

THOMSON
™
WADSWORTH

BUSINESS REPLY MAIL
FIRST-CLASS MAIL   PERMIT NO. 34   BELMONT CA

POSTAGE WILL BE PAID BY ADDRESSEE

Attn: Michele Sordi, Sr. Editor, Psychology

Thomson Wadsworth

10 Davis Drive

Belmont, CA   94002-9801

IIhIhIIhIIhIIhIhIIhIhIhIhIhIhIIhIhIIhIhIIhIhII

FOLD HERE

OPTIONAL:

Your name: _____ Date: _____

May we quote you, either in promotion for *An Invitation to Social Psychology: Expressing and Censoring the Self*, or in future publishing ventures?

Yes: _____   No: _____